# 50 LESSONS FOR LAWYERS

# 50 LESSONS FOR LAWYERS

*Earn more. Stress less. Be awesome.*

NORA RIVA BERGMAN

50 Lessons for Lawyers
Earn more. Stress less. Be awesome.

Copyright © 2016 Nora Riva Bergman

Berroco Canyon Publishing
All rights reserved.

ISBN-13: 9780997263701
ISBN-10: 0997263709
Library of Congress Control Number: 2016906419
Berroco Canyon Publishing, Tarpon Springs, FL

# ABOUT THE AUTHOR

A licensed attorney since 1992, Nora Riva Bergman is a law firm coach who understands the unique challenges lawyers face in the 21st century. She has practiced as an employment law attorney and certified mediator and has served as an adjunct professor at both Stetson University College of Law and the University of South Florida.

Nora has been a speaker at conferences for the American Bar Association, the Federal Bar Association, the American Academy of Adoption Attorneys, the National Association of Bar Executives, The Florida Bar, and other national and regional legal organizations. She also served for eight years as the executive director of a voluntary bar association with over 1,200 members.

She is certified in the Conflict Dynamics Profile developed by the Center for Conflict Dynamics at Eckerd College to help individuals and organizations learn to deal constructively with conflict. Nora is also a graduate of Villanova University's Lean Six Sigma Program and is certified in both DISC and EQ through Target Training International. Since 2012, she has been member of the Thought Leader Team at Law Without Walls, an international program for law students founded by the University of Miami School of Law.

Nora received an undergraduate degree in journalism, *summa cum laude*, from the University of South Florida and her JD, *cum laude*, from Stetson University College of Law, where she was a member of the law review and served as a mentor for incoming students.

# TABLE OF CONTENTS

# FOREWORD

I hope you can take the time to absorb and execute on the lessons in this book. It is filled with gems about how to take control of your day, minimize unwanted interruptions, reduce stress, build a great team, and love your practice again. If you apply only twenty percent of these tips, they will change your life forever. Before I take a moment to discuss the book, let me say a bit about the author.

I met Nora in 2005 and personally recruited her to join our company. Atticus is the market leader in coaching successful attorneys who are committed to being the best. To achieve that goal, we have to find great coaches who can live up to the demands of successful attorneys. Let's face it, in addition to being highly intelligent, most attorneys are also a bit critical in their thinking (if not cynical at times) and argumentative when necessary. Not everyone, regardless of their knowledge can stand toe-to-toe with a hard-charging, powerful attorney when that attorney doesn't want to hear what you have to say. In Nora, I immediately saw the type of leader I was looking for. I saw the commitment to make a difference for the legal community, someone who understood the pain that lawyers deal with every day, the compassion to listen and the courage to speak straight. She has lived up to those first impressions, becoming a great coach for lawyers around the country.

Nora is also uniquely qualified to address the lessons that every lawyer needs to learn to have a successful practice and a fulfilled life. She has been in the trenches as a practicing attorney. She has seen and lived the struggles that most every attorney confronts in building a practice. She has been the executive director of a voluntary bar association and has seen the challenges lawyers face every day. She's seen what can happen to attorneys who haven't learned some of the lessons in this book: the out of balance lives, illnesses caused by stress, alcoholism, depression and even suicide. For the past ten years Nora has been helping attorneys reconnect with their purpose and achieve their goals as a Certified Practice Advisor with Atticus.

So, I love tips, and Nora has laid out great ones in these lessons. But the truth is, if you're like most attorneys, you're not good at executing. If I may make a suggestion: read the book, circle the lessons that you would be willing to experiment with and implement five of them over a 90-day period. Watch what happens – how your practice and your life improve over those 90 days. Then take on another five lessons and do the same thing. You will have a life-altering, practice-altering experience. If you try this method, and at the end of 90 days you have not implemented the lessons…call Nora! She is an expert at getting results, ensuring that you implement, and that you do change your life.

Nora's commitment is to help you change your life. What's your commitment?

Mark Powers
Founder and President of Atticus

## ACKNOWLEDGMENTS

*I'm doing my best to live what I teach.*

— MAYA ANGELOU

That quote from Maya Angelou sits on my desk where I can see it every day. It is a wonderful reminder that we are all works in progress. Each day we have the opportunity to be just a little bit better than we were the day before. 50 Lessons for Lawyers is designed help you in your journey.

This book is a compilation of lessons I've learned over the past 25 years – lessons I learned as a practicing attorney, lessons I learned working with attorneys as the executive director of a voluntary bar association, and lessons I have learned – *and continue to learn* – from clients and colleagues as a business coach. This book is a tribute and a thank you to everyone who has taught me and helped me to live what I teach. I also share lessons I've learned from more than 70 books. I recommend each and every book I've cited. They have changed my life.

*There is nothing to writing. All you do is*
*sit down at a typewriter and bleed.*

— ERNEST HEMINGWAY

I feel that saying I wrote this book isn't exactly right. Yes, I wrote the words down. But so many people were part of the process, whether they know it or not. That being said, there are a few people who truly made this book possible.

When Mark Powers asked me to become a Practice Advisor with Atticus, it changed my life. No hyperbole here. It changed my life. Over the years, people have asked me, "Why did you go from being a bar association executive to a business coach for lawyers?" That's easy. My favorite aspect of being a bar executive was having the opportunity to help other lawyers. As a business coach for lawyers, having the opportunity to help other lawyers is why I do what I do. Thank you, Mark, for encouraging me to follow this path.

Thank you to all my clients. The clients I represented when I practiced law taught me what it means to be a lawyer. The clients I have worked with as a business coach inspire me every day to "do my best to live what I teach."

*50 Lessons for Lawyers* would not be a reality without the efforts of the great team I've had the privilege of working with on this project. Thank you to my editor, David Wasserstrom, whose input and insights were invaluable. Thank you, David, for your ideas, suggestions, and thoughtful comments. Brian Frolo designed the *50 Lessons for Lawyers* logo and helped integrate the lessons into my website. Thank you, Brian, for your insights, meticulous attention to detail, your incredible eye for design, and, of course, your friendship. Melody Jones has worked with me for several years as a social media and marketing assistant. Thank you, Melody, for helping me keep all the balls in air.

Thank you to my mom and dad and my Aunt Riva who, although they are no longer on this planet, have influenced every page of this book. Finally, thank you to my partner in life for over 32 years, Jan Rouse. If not for Jan's love and support and encouragement I may never have gone to college, let alone law school! More than anyone else in my life, Jan has loved me, put up with me, and helped me to be just a little bit better each day than I was the day before.

Nora Riva Bergman
August 31, 2016

# HOW TO USE THIS BOOK

*Believe nothing just because a so-called wise person said it. Believe nothing just because a belief is generally held. Believe nothing just because it is said in ancient books. Believe nothing just because it is said to be of divine origin. Believe nothing just because someone else believes it. Believe only what you yourself test and judge to be true.*

— ATTRIBUTED TO THE BUDDHA

*50 Lessons for Lawyers* is written for lawyers, but you don't have to be a lawyer to learn the lessons and apply them to your life. The lessons are relevant to anyone who wants to earn more and stress less. If you actually start living just one of the lessons, it will change your life for the better.

*50 Lessons for Lawyers* can be read in any way you like. You can read all of the lessons sequentially or you can start with any lesson that resonates with you. You don't have to start with Lesson 1., but I recommend it. Lesson 1. provides the foundation for all of the lessons that follow. It's a good place to start. Also, you'll notice that many of the lessons cite other lessons, so it's OK to jump around if you want to.

You might want to use *50 Lessons for Lawyers* as your own one-year course on self-improvement by reading (and applying!) one lesson each week over the course of a year. Think of each lesson as a new habit and focus on creating that habit. You may want to spend more than one week on a particular lesson, and that's OK, too.

While all 50 Lessons are important, you may feel that some are more relevant to you than others. I'm betting that you may already "know" some of what the lessons teach. But as you'll learn in Lesson 2., there is a big difference between "knowing" and "doing."

*50 Lessons for Lawyers* draws on the knowledge and research of more than 70 other books and a variety of online resources. Each book referenced is cited at the end of each lesson. I am indebted to the authors cited herein for the lessons they have taught me through their writing.

Finally, each lesson ends with a section entitled Living the Lesson. Living the Lesson provides suggestions on how to apply the lesson to your practice and your life. Living the Lesson helps you move from knowing – to – doing.

Here's to the journey!

*Lesson 1*

●  ●  ●  ●

## THIS IS YOUR LIFE. ARE YOU LIVING IT OR IS IT LIVING YOU?

*How we spend our days is, of course, how we spend our lives.*

*— ANNIE DILLARD*

How are you spending your days? If you're like most lawyers, you're too busy putting out fires to worry about how you're spending your days. You're too busy paying the bills. You're too busy dealing with staff. You're too busy arguing with opposing counsel – or sometimes, your clients.

But then something happens: A loved one dies unexpectedly, or perhaps you're diagnosed with a serious illness. Everything changes. It often takes a life crisis to wake us up and force us to examine how we're spending our days. I think of these times in our lives as ampersands: Before the event & after the event. Everything changes after the ampersand. There is the "before" & "after."

Maybe you've lived through ampersands that have forced you to change some aspect of your life. But most of us don't have ampersands that force us to change our working behavior. Instead, too many lawyers are stuck in work, work, work mode, unaware of what's going on around them. Or we attempt to change time after time, with little success. We walk into the office on any given Monday morning and say, "Today will be different!" And yet it never is. But today can be different. And since you're here, reading this now, I think you know it can be different. The good news is that you're right. You can change your life for the better – one step at a time. One lesson at a time.

My vision is that each one of these 50 Lessons will be an ampersand for you. The 50 lessons that follow focus on skills to develop, habits to create (and habits to extinguish), and strategies that simply are not taught in law school. My hope for you is that you don't just read the 50 Lessons. My hope is that you live them. By living the 50 Lessons, you'll be able to create a law practice that serves your life, rather than living a life that serves your law practice. Let's get started.

*If today were the last day of your life, would you*
*want to do what you are about to do today?*

*— STEVE JOBS*

This first lesson is the most important lesson, because if you don't realize that this is your life and begin taking control of it, your life will live you. Start by getting very clear about what you want from your life – both personally and professionally. Write your thoughts down. Call it a "Mission Statement" or a "Vision Statement" or "My Manifesto." Call it whatever you like. It doesn't matter WHAT you call it. What matters is that you KNOW what you want. What matters is that you KNOW why you do what you do. I would suggest creating a personal mission first, then creating a professional mission. Your law practice should serve your life, not the other way around.

*A year from now, you may wish you had started today.*

*— KAREN LAMB*

Without a clear understanding of what you want from your life, both personally and professionally, you will forever be living your life by default, rather than by design. In the business classic, *The 7 Habits of Highly Effective People*,[1:1] Stephen Covey talks about the importance of seeing the "big picture" of your life as a starting point against which all of your actions are measured. He refers to this as "beginning with the end in mind."

> To begin with the end in mind means to start with a clear understanding of your destination. It means to know where you're going so that you better understand where you are now and so that the steps you take are always in the right direction.
> – From *The 7 Habits of Highly Effective People*

Your mission is the compass that keeps you moving in the right direction. That is why it is the focus of this first lesson. Your mission statement doesn't need to be lengthy. In fact, the shorter the better. Think of your mission statement like the United States Constitution. It is the document against which all of your actions are measured. And remember, simplicity is an asset. There are only 272 words in the Gettysburg Address.

When you have a clear mission for your life, it will become the means by which you determine how you "spend your days" and in turn, how you spend your life.

> *Write down on paper your goal in life. You cannot find happiness until your goal is clear and in view.*
>
> – ROSS BYRON

## LIVING THE LESSON

* Create a mission statement for both your personal life and your professional life.
* Start by creating your personal mission. Your personal mission should drive your professional mission – not the other way around.

aside a few hours and go somewhere where you can focus and ɾ be distracted. Bring pen and paper or a tablet or iPad – whatever works for you. For help getting started and to view sample mission statements, go to:

www.missionstatements.com.

* After creating your personal mission, use it as a guide to inform your professional mission. Writing your personal mission will help you discover those things that are most important to you. Use what you discover as the starting point for your professional mission.

* If you run your own law firm, you should create a mission statement for your firm in the same way you created your personal and professional mission statements.

* Keep copies of your mission statements close by. Keep your personal mission on a card in your wallet or on your phone. Keep your professional mission on your desk in your office where you can see it every day. Display your firm's mission on your website and in your reception area so that it can serve as a source of motivation for you and your staff, and as a source of inspiration for your clients.

*20 years from now you will be more disappointed by the things you didn't do than by the ones you did. So throw off the bowlines. Sail away from the safe harbor. Catch the trade winds in your sails. Explore. Dream. Discover.*

*– MARK TWAIN*

[1:1] Covey, Stephen R. (1989, 2004). *The 7 Habits of Highly Effective People.* Simon & Schuster.

## Lesson 2

●  ●  ●  ●

# UNDERSTAND THE DIFFERENCE BETWEEN KNOWING AND DOING. START DOING.

*The future depends on what we do in the present.*

– GANDHI

The wisdom in Gandhi's quote seems so obvious. So simple. Yet, as you'll discover throughout the 50 Lessons, simple does not mean easy.

Think about Gandhi's quote for a moment. He doesn't say: The future depends on what we *know* in the present – or what we *think* in the present. The future, as Gandhi so eloquently states, depends on what we *do* in the present.

The "simple" things often are things we already "know." But there can be an enormous gap between "knowing" and "doing." You know you should eat right. You know you should exercise regularly. You know you should get enough rest. You know you should start working on that brief that's due in two weeks. But what are you *doing?* Doing is what counts. And doing something requires…well…doing something.

All too often we confuse knowing – or talking – with doing. Knowing what to do or talking about what you are going to do is not doing it. Would you get on an airplane if the person in the cockpit *knows* how to fly and can *talk* to you about it, but has never actually *done* it? In their book, *The Knowing-Doing Gap*,[2:1] authors Jeffrey Pfeffer and Robert Sutton explain that while planning and strategizing are important functions in any organization, they often become a substitute for action.

One of the main barriers to turning knowledge into action is the tendency to treat talking about something as equivalent to actually doing something about it. Talking about what should be done, writing plans about what an organization should do, and collecting and analyzing data to help decide what actions to take can guide and motivate action. Indeed, rhetoric frequently is an essential first step toward taking action. But just talking about what to do isn't enough. Nor is planning for the future enough to produce that future. Something has to get done, and someone has to do it.

– From *The Knowing-Doing Gap*

Planning is important, but as Pfeffer and Sutton note, "Action counts more than elegant plans and concepts." Create your plan, then act on it. Period.

So now you *know* about the knowing-doing gap. But that's not enough. You must *do* something about it. How do you move from knowing to doing, both personally and with respect to your business? First, recognize habits that may be keeping you from taking action. (More about habits in Lesson 4. Get rid of bad habits. 90% of our behavior is based on our habits, and Lesson 5. Create 12 new GOOD habits each year.) Next, understand that *any action is better than none*. Rosabeth Moss Kanter explains four reasons why in a post from the HBR Blog Network.[2:2]

1. **Small wins matter**. Small wins pave the way for big wins. In her book, *Confidence*,[2:3] Kanter studied numerous business turnarounds and sports teams. Her research showed that confidence – "the

expectation of a positive outcome" – built by small wins was a big reason for success.

2.  **Accomplishments come in pieces.** One of my favorite sayings is: "You can't jump to the top of Mount Everest." You must take one step at a time – one action at a time. Incremental change can produce monumental results.

3.  **Forget perfection.** The desire for perfection is one of the biggest reasons people procrastinate. They put off getting started because the outcome may not be perfect. So what? Start. Do. You can strive for perfection as you go along.

4.  **Actions produce energy and momentum.** While overwork can produce stress, many studies have shown that the more control we feel, the less stress we feel. (*See* Lesson 3. TANSTATM! There ain't no such thing as time management.) Focused action will help you take more control over your life and your practice.

In his book, *The E-Myth Revisited,*[2:4] author Michael Gerber recounts a story about Tom Watson, the founder of IBM, who explained the phenomenal early success of the company.

> *IBM is what it is today for three special reasons. The first reason is that, at the very beginning, I had a very clear picture of what the company would look like when it was finally done. You might say I had a model in my mind of what it would look like when the dream -- my vision -- was in place.*
>
> *The second reason was that once I had that picture, I then asked myself how a company which looks like that would have to act. I then created a picture of how IBM would act when it was finally done.*
>
> *The third reason IBM has been so successful was that once I had a picture of how IBM would look when the dream was in place and how such a company would have to act, I then realized that, unless we began to act that way from the very beginning, we would never get there.*

*In other words, I realized that for IBM to become a great company,
it would have to act like a great company long before it ever became one.*

Watson is talking about the power of acting "as if" you've already achieved
your goals. Once you know what you want and where you want to be, start
acting today "as if" you're already there. You will be astounded at the changes
you will see in your life. Dare to be great! Create your vision, then take action.
Live it. Starting now. Just like IBM.

## LIVING THE LESSON

* Commit to doing at least three things every day that are consistent
  with your mission and move you toward your goals.
* Keep a "Journal of Three" to track your actions. Write down your
  actions as you do them each day. Remember, actions create energy
  and momentum. Keeping a journal will help you capitalize on that
  momentum and will also remind you of just how much you've
  accomplished.
* Don't wait to be the person you want to be. Don't wait to create the
  law firm you envision. Start today. Act "as if" you're already there,
  and you'll arrive much sooner.

*Being busy does not always mean real work. The
object of all work is production or accomplishment
and to either of these ends there must be forethought,
system, planning, intelligence, and honest purpose, as
well as perspiration. Seeming to do is not doing.*

— THOMAS A. EDISON

[2:1] Sutton, Robert I. and Pfeffer, Jeffrey (1999). *The Knowing-Doing Gap:
How Smart Companies Turn Knowledge Into Action*. Perseus Books Group.

[2:2] Kanter, Rosabeth Moss. *Four Reasons Any Action Is Better Than None* (2011). Retrieved from http://blogs.hbr.org/kanter/2011/03/four-reasons-any-action-is-bet.html

[2:3] Kanter, Rosabeth Moss. *Confidence* (2006). Crown Business.

[2:4] Gerber, Michael (2009). *The E-Myth Revisited*. HarperCollins.

*Lesson 3*

●　　●　　●　　●

# TANSTATM! THERE AIN'T NO SUCH THING AS TIME MANAGEMENT.

*It's not enough to be busy. So are the ants. The
question is: What are we busy about?*

— HENRY DAVID THOREAU

We use the phrase "time management" because we've been conditioned to do so over the years. But there really is no such thing as time management. Once you understand that you cannot manage time – you can only manage yourself – you'll begin to *think* differently about time. And when you begin to think differently about time, you'll begin to *act* differently. And until you begin to act differently, you'll never be able to take *control* of your calendar or your life.

It has always been a badge of honor for lawyers to work ridiculously long hours. The law firm culture says work late, every night, no matter what you are working on. Oh, and come in on weekends, too. This is a recipe for stress and burn-out. Moreover, research shows that those long hours may be jeopardizing your health.

A study from Health.com and reported by CNN found that "people who work more than 10 hours a day are about 60 percent more likely to develop heart disease or have a heart attack than people who clock just seven hours a day." According to Marianna Virtanen, M.D., doctors "should include working long hours in their list of potential risk factors" for heart disease. And Peter Kaufmann, Ph.D., says that people who are driven and impatient at work "may be equally driven and impatient with…family and friends."

As Tony Schwartz, author and founder of The Energy Project notes in an article he wrote for the Harvard Business Review online:

> Just as you'll eventually go broke if you make constant withdrawals from your bank account without offsetting deposits, you will also ultimately burn yourself out if you spend too much energy too continuously at work without sufficient renewal…When you're running as fast as you can, what you sacrifice is attention to detail, and time to step back, reflect on the big picture, and truly think strategically and long-term.[3:1]

*Control = less stress*

## A BIT OF HISTORY

In 1954, Julian B. Rotter created the theory of "locus of control." In a nutshell, the locus of control theory states that, as individuals, we either have an internal or external locus of control. Those who have an external locus of control tend to see themselves as having no ability to control their own lives. They are buffeted by the four winds and drift wherever those winds take them. Their lives are incredibly stressful because they believe they have little control over what happens to them. Conversely, individuals with an internal locus of control believe they can control their lives and their destinies.

Here's a simple way to think about the relationship between stress and control: The level of stress we feel is inversely proportionate to the level of control we feel we have over our lives. Less control; more stress. More control; less stress.

Fortunately, there are things you can do to increase your internal locus of control. Though it may sound like a paradox, you can increase your internal locus of control by exercising more control over your life.

## ADRENALINE ADDICTION

While research has proven that the more control we have over our lives the less stress we feel, the truth is, many attorneys like stress – and lots of it. Have you ever said to yourself, "I work best under pressure," or "I'm really deadline driven"? Can you go for more than five minutes without checking your phone? Do you find yourself checking your email in the middle of the night? Do you run from meeting to meeting with no time in between? Do you feel as though you always "over-promise" and "under-deliver"? Do you always feel overwhelmed? Are you usually running late? Do you arrive at the office already feeling rushed?

These are just a few of the telltale signs of adrenaline addiction. And many lawyers suffer from it. Adrenaline is the most potent stimulant created by our sympathetic nervous system. It's created in response to stress and increases heart rate, pulse rate, and blood pressure. It also raises the blood levels of glucose and lipids, in addition to having other metabolic effects on us. We are not built to have adrenaline coursing through our veins all or most of the time. Unfortunately, that's exactly what happens to adrenaline addicts.

In his article, *The Painful Reality of Adrenaline Addiction*,[3:2] Patrick Lencioni, explains:

> There is something particularly insidious about adrenaline addiction that makes it hard for many leaders to kick the habit. Unlike other addicts whose behaviors are socially frowned-upon, adrenaline addicts are often praised for their frantic activity, even promoted for it during their careers. And so they often wear their problem like a badge of honor, failing to see it as an addiction at all in spite of the pain it causes. When confronted about their problem, adrenaline addicts (I'm a recovering one myself) will tell you about their endless list of responsibilities and all the people who need their attention. And while they'll often complain about their situation, they'll quickly brush off any constructive advice from spouses, friends or co-workers who "just don't understand."

The legal profession has a long history of encouraging adrenaline addiction. How many lawyers have you heard brag about the long hours they work? Maybe you're one of them. If you are, then it's time to make some changes. The first step is to change your thinking. Refuse to accept the myths that say, "There just aren't enough hours in the day," or "I have no control over my time." There really is enough time, and you can take control.

> *Don't say you don't have enough time. You have exactly the same number of hours per day that were given to Helen Keller, Pasteur, Michelangelo, Mother Theresa, Leonardo da Vinci, Thomas Jefferson, and Albert Einstein.*
>
> *– H. JACKSON BROWNE*

As a lawyer, you are a member of one of the most important professions on the planet. You may not think about it often, but lawyers are life-changers. The work lawyers do transforms people's lives. Forget the lawyer jokes; the work you do makes a difference for your clients, your community and our world. But it's your responsibility to manage yourself around the time you have. As a lawyer, you've been given the opportunity to make a difference. Don't gripe about not having enough time to get it all done. Instead, make a conscious choice to say "no" to those things that are not important. If you know your mission and strive to live it, you'll become much better at saying "no" to the unimportant things. Give your very best time and talents to those things you are passionate about.

## LIVING THE LESSON

* Change your "time management" mindset. Think in terms of "self-management."
* Increase your locus of control by taking more control of your calendar. Identify those things that you need to do each day or each week

and schedule the time in your calendar. For example, if you want to meet with your key people each day, schedule those meetings in your calendar and treat them just as you would treat an appointment with a client.

* If you find that you are always working late, make a commitment to leave the office by 5:30 p.m. at least two days a week. Your loved ones want to see you.

[3:1] Schwartz, Tony. *The Productivity Myth* (2010). Retrieved from https://hbr.org/2010/05/the-productivity-myth-2
[3:2] Lencioni, Patrick. The Painful Reality of Adrenaline Addiction (2004). Retrieved from http://www.tablegroup.com/blog/the-painful-reality-of-adrenaline-addiction

*Lesson 4*

● ● ● ●

# GET RID OF BAD HABITS.
# 90% OF OUR BEHAVIOR IS BASED ON OUR HABITS.

*Insanity is doing the same thing, over and over
again, and expecting different results.*

*— ALBERT EINSTEIN*

If you think about bad habits, aren't they the living definition of insanity? As psychologist and philosopher William James wrote in the late 19th century, we are "mere bundles of habits." My friend, Mark Powers, the founder and president of Atticus, a coaching and consulting firm that works exclusively with attorneys, likes to tell the story of the lawyer who's trying to change his work habits:

You get up in the morning and say to yourself, "TODAY is the day! TODAY I will get to the office and work through my "to do" list. TODAY is the day! TODAY I will start to take control of my calendar. TODAY I will go home in time to have dinner with my family." But at seven o'clock, you're still at your desk and, once again, you feel like you've worked all day with little to show for it. "Oh well," you say to yourself, "Tomorrow is another day."

The lawyer in Mark's story is like so many of us. We know we should change, and we truly want to change. But we are prisoners of our habits. These 50 Lessons will challenge you to examine your habits so that you can identify which habits work for you and pull you toward your goals, and which habits hold you back.

*✭ acknowledge what isn't working ✭*

## YOU ARE HERE.

The first step in changing your bad habits is acknowledging that what you're doing isn't working. If you're reading this, you know it's time to start doing things differently. It's time for a change. So, let's look at how the process of change works. In *Changing for Good*,[4:1] the authors explain the process of change in six stages. Each stage is part of the change process, which they define as: "Any activity that you initiate to help modify your thinking, feeling, or behavior." Written from a clinical psychology perspective, *Changing for Good* is grounded in research on how individuals have overcome addictive behaviors such as smoking. Its lessons, however, offer valuable guidance to anyone who wants to rid themselves of a bad habit, such as working until all hours of the night when you'd rather be home with your family. (Yes, that is a habit.)

Following are the Six Stages of Change outlined in *Changing for Good*. By understanding where you are on the continuum of change, you can take actions that move you to the next stage.

**Precontemplation:** Precontemplators don't see any need to change, and thus resist it. But while most pre-contemplators don't want to change themselves, they'd love to change everyone else. Often they avoid even thinking about their problems because they feel the situation is hopeless. If your loved ones have told you that you're working too much, listen to them, and move out of this stage

**Contemplation:** Contemplators want to stop feeling stuck. They want to change, but they are always looking for a better solution to their problem. According to the authors, "People who eternally substitute thinking for action can be called chronic contemplators." I'd say they're stuck in the knowing-doing gap. (*See* Lesson 2. Understand the difference between knowing and doing. Start doing.)

**Preparation:** People in the preparation stage are committed to action. If you are in the preparation stage, it's the time to publicize your change efforts. In your office, this can be as simple as telling your assistant that beginning on Monday, you plan to leave the office at 5:30 p.m. each day. Enlist the help of those around you to move you to the next phase – action.

**Action:** This is where the rubber meets the road, and you actually change your behavior. Remember that while this stage exhibits the most visible form of change, "…it is far from the only one; you can also change your level of awareness, your emotions, your self-image, your thinking, and so on. And many of those changes take place in the stages that precede action."

**Maintenance:** In this stage, you begin to consolidate the gains you've made so that your changes become permanent. Without a strong commitment to maintenance, you'll likely go back to your old ways. *But remember: Action followed by a return to bad habits is better than no action at all.* Research shows that most people who quit smoking report three or four unsuccessful attempts before they succeed. The lesson? Don't get discouraged! As you begin to live the 50 Lessons, you might fall back into old habits as you start to build new ones. Don't beat yourself up about it! Just get back on the horse! You'll get there.

**Termination:** At this point, you've extinguished the habit.

As you move through these stages, don't get discouraged. Changing bad habits isn't easy. But it's worth it. Just get started. Take action!

Action followed by relapse is far better than no action at all. People who take action and fail in the next month are twice as likely to succeed over the next six months than those who don't take any action at all.
– From *Changing for Good*

## HOW JUST 20 SECONDS CAN HELP YOU CHANGE HABITS

Just as it takes tremendous initial thrust for a rocket to break through the bounds of gravity, changing a habit always requires a fair amount of initial energy. Why? According to Shawn Achor, author of *The Happiness Advantage: The Seven Principles of Positive Psychology That Fuel Success and Performance at Work*,[4:2] it is because "...we are drawn to those things that are easy, convenient and habitual, and it is incredibly difficult to overcome this inertia." Achor's book catalogs the neuroscience behind positive psychology and outlines seven principles for upping your competitive advantage by upping your happiness quotient. That may sound like mushy, right-brain, mumbo-jumbo to most left-brain lawyers, but the principles in *The Happiness Advantage* are grounded in thousands of scientific studies, as well as in Achor's own research on 1,600 Harvard University students and dozens of Fortune 500 companies.

One of Achor's seven principles is something he calls "The 20-Second Rule." The concept is simple and effective: If you want to get rid of a bad habit, make it more difficult to engage in it. If you want to stop your habit of eating chocolate ice cream at 11 o'clock at night, don't keep any in your freezer. You're much less likely to get in your car in the middle of the night to buy ice cream than you are to saunter into your kitchen and down a pint of Ben and Jerry's that's waiting in your freezer. Research shows that making it even slightly more difficult to engage in a bad habit can help you extinguish it.

The same principle works at the office. Let's use the example of habitually checking email throughout the day. According to Tim Burress, co-author of several books on effective email habits, the average professional spends about two-and-a-half to three hours per day on email. If you want to break yourself of the habit of habitually checking your email, turn it off and only check your email at certain times during the day. You will be amazed at how much more focused and productive you'll be.

## LIVING THE LESSON

* Know that wherever you are in the process of change, you can do it.
* Identify those habits that you want to extinguish.
* Use the "The 20-Second Rule" to begin to change your habits.
* Start small. Extinguishing just one unproductive habit can make a huge impact over time.

[4:1] Norcross, John C., Prochaska, James O. and DiClemente, Carlo C. (2010). *Changing for Good: A Revolutionary Six-Stage Program for Overcoming Bad Habits and Moving Your Life Positively Forward.* HarperCollins.
[4:2] Achor, Shawn (2010). *The Happiness Advantage: The Seven Principles of Positive Psychology That Fuel Success and Performance at Work.* Crown Business.

*—Set a daily schedule every day when you get to the office*

*Lesson 5*

● ● ● ●

# CREATE 12 NEW GOOD HABITS EACH YEAR.

*We are what we repeatedly do. Excellence,*
*then, is not an act but a habit.*

*— ARISTOTLE*

Habits are powerful things. They can either pull us toward a positive future or anchor us to our past. Think about that for a moment. The habits you have in your life right now were created in the past, but they exert a powerful force on your future because, as Gandhi said, "The future depends on what we do in the present." What you are doing right now is creating your future. And since up to 90% of our behavior is based on habit, our habits control what we do in the present.

So much of what you do every day is habit — from brushing your teeth each morning, to the route you drive to work, to where you stop for coffee, to how you take your coffee, to what you do when you first get to the office. You get the idea. Habits are the autopilot that guides our brains. So creating habits around the things we want to do is the best way to make sure that those things get done. As crazy as it may sound, the less you have to think about doing something, the more likely you are to actually do it. As William James once wrote, habit "…is the reason why we do a thing with difficulty the first time, but soon do it more and more easily, and finally, with sufficient practice, do it semi-mechanically, or with hardly any consciousness at all."

## BUT I'VE JUST GOT TO CHECK MY EMAIL NOW!

Most lawyers have some really bad habits that destroy their focus, decrease their productivity, and smack down their earning potential. Ouch. But changing our habits isn't easy. (*See* Lesson 4. Get rid of bad habits. 90% of our behavior is based on our habits.) Before we talk about creating new habits, let's look at how habits are created.

According to Charles Duhigg, author of *The Power of Habit: Why We Do What We Do in Life and Business*,[5:1] habits are created by combining 1) a cue; 2) a routine; and 3) a reward, then cultivating a craving that drives the habit loop. In Lesson 4, I recommended the "20 Second Rule" as one way to break a bad habit by simply making the habit more difficult to engage in. Now, let's look at how the habit loop works with respect to creating the habit in the first place. Imagine this scene:

> You're working on the motion that's due next Friday. As you're reviewing your expert's deposition, you hear the "ding" of your computer or phone (the cue) letting you know "You've got mail!" Your brain starts anticipating the distraction (the reward) of checking your email. "That could be important," you think to yourself. So you stop what you're doing to check your email every time you hear the "ding." When the anticipation of the reward of momentary distraction becomes so strong that it is a *craving* – i.e., you must have it – a habit is born.

To create a new habit, we need to recognize that the craving drives our behavior. In the example above, the craving is for the reward of distraction. So how do we stop the craving? Take away the cue. Turn off your email and phone when you want to focus.

Most of the time, these cravings emerge so gradually that we're not really aware they exist, so we're often blind to their influence. But as we associate cues with certain rewards, a subconscious craving emerges in our brains that starts the habit loop spinning.

    – From *The Power of Habit*

The trick is to create an environment that rewards us for the right behavior, rather than those behaviors that work against us.

[W]e must make automatic and habitual, as early as possible, as many useful actions as we can…The more of the details of our daily life we can hand over to the effortless custody of automatism, the more our higher powers of mind will be set free for their own proper work. There is no more miserable human being than one in whom nothing is habitual but indecision, and for whom the lighting of every cigar, the drinking of every cup, the time of rising and going to bed every day, and the beginning of every bit of work are subjects of express volitional deliberation.

    – From *The Principles of Psychology (1890), by William James*[5:2]

## LIVING THE LESSON

There are essentially three steps to creating a new habit. Follow these steps, and you can create new, powerful habits that pull you toward your goals rather than holding you back. The steps are simple. *Caveat: Simple doesn't mean easy.*

* Decide on the habit you want to create, and be as specific as possible. A habit of "drinking more water" is problematic, whereas a habit of "drinking six glasses a day" is easier to create. Creating the habit of checking your email "less often" is not as effective as creating the habit of checking your email "once in the morning, and once in the afternoon."

* Set up cues or triggers to help you remember the action at the time you want to do it. During the time before the action becomes a habit (usually the first few weeks), you will need to use external triggers or reminders. For example, if you want to make it a habit to meet with your paralegal each day, put the meeting in your calendar. You'll need the reminder until the meetings – or huddles – become a habit. (More about huddles in Lesson 10. Put an end to "lurk and blurt" with huddles.)

* Make it easy to remember what you are trying to do. Rituals and routines support remembering. For example, if you want to create the habit of meditating for five minutes each morning, do it in the same place, at the same time, and in the same surroundings each day. (More about the power of meditation in Lesson 13. Do the harder thing first.) For example, I've created my own morning meditation ritual that incorporates my Starbucks habit. (Yes, I consider this to be a good habit!) Each morning, I go to my neighborhood Starbucks before I begin my work day. I get my coffee to take back to my office. But when I get in my car, rather than leaving immediately, I sit for five to 10 minutes and listen to a guided meditation on my iPhone. Doors locked, windows up, headphones on, phone in airplane mode so that I can't be interrupted. This ritual works for me. Find rituals that work for you.

[5:1] Duhigg, Charles (2012). *The Power of Habit: Why We Do What We Do in Life and Business*. Random House.
[5:2] James, William (1890). *The Principles of Psychology*. London, England: Macmillan and Co.

*Lesson 6*

●　●　●　●

# UNDERSTAND AND APPLY THE POWER OF FOCUS.

*That's been one of my mantras — focus and simplicity. Simple*
*can be harder than complex: You have to work hard to get*
*your thinking clean to make it simple. But it's worth it in the*
*end because once you get there, you can move mountains.*

*— STEVE JOBS*

When was the last time you felt as though you were able to give one hundred percent of your attention to a particular task? If you're like most lawyers, your answer is probably something like, "I can't really remember," or "Not often enough." It doesn't matter what you're working on, there is always something else clamoring for attention. And the more things we have clamoring for our attention, the less attention we have. More than one of my clients has said to me, "You know, I feel like I have ADD." And the reality is that many, or more likely most, lawyers suffer from self-induced ADD. And lawyers are not alone.

Below is a listing of the symptoms or criteria for diagnosis of ADD from the *DSM-IV Diagnostic and Statistical Manual of Mental Disorders of the American Psychiatric Association*: [6:1]

* Often fails to give close attention to details or makes careless mistakes in schoolwork, work or other activities
* Often has difficulty sustaining attention in tasks or play activities
* Often does not seem to listen when spoken to directly
* Often does not follow through on instructions and fails to finish schoolwork, chores, or duties in the workplace
* Often has difficulty organizing tasks and activities
* Often avoids, dislikes, or is reluctant to engage in tasks or activities that require sustained mental effort
* Often loses things necessary for tasks or activities
* Often easily distracted by extraneous stimuli
* Often forgetful in daily activities

Sound familiar? Painfully familiar? Psychiatrist Edward M. Hallowell, who specializes in the diagnosis and treatment of ADD, says that he has come to see ADD as a "metaphor for modern life." In his book, *CrazyBusy*, [6:2] Hallowell notes that, "...once applicable to only a relative few, the symptoms of ADD now seem to describe just about everybody." The pull of the email "ding," the ringing phone, the text message, the Facebook notification, the CNN news update, all conspire to create a sense that you must pay attention to everything. But what ends up happening is that by trying to pay attention to everything, you slowly lose the ability to pay attention to anything.

## SO HOW DID WE GET TO THIS POINT?

In an interview with *Harvard Business Review*,[6:3] Maggie Jackson, author of *Distracted: The Erosion of Attention and the Coming Dark Age*,[6:4] says that the self-induced ADD so many of us deal with didn't start in the digital age. "[I]t goes back to inventions from 150-200 years ago and the new experiences of time and space they provided us...The possibility of doing two or more things at once has long intrigued us," Jackson says. Jackson recognizes that there are times when we need to multitask, but we also must develop our attention skills fully. The problem is, most of us spend much more time multitasking than we do working to develop our attention skills. As Hallowell explains in *CrazyBusy*, multitasking is like playing tennis with two balls. Imagine trying to focus on two balls at one time. You'd be running all over the place. And even if you could keep two balls in play at one time, you couldn't do it for long. You just can't keep your eye on two balls at one time and expect to perform well.

## WHAT YOU CAN DO TO IMPROVE YOUR FOCUS:

The good news is that there are things you can do to improve your focus. Some are simple exercises you can perform at your desk, and others are lifestyle changes. Taken together, they will make a huge impact on your ability to focus.

## REDUCE MULTITASKING.

Too much multitasking – or as it is more aptly called, "switchtasking" – is one of the biggest impediments to increasing our focus. The truth is, our brains cannot multitask. They can only focus on one thing at a time. And as we age, our ability to switch quickly from one task to another diminishes. Maybe you've experienced this first-hand by accidentally hitting "Reply to All" in an email while talking on the phone and processing emails at the same time.

Research conducted by the University of London found that workers who are distracted by email and phone calls can suffer a 10-point drop in IQ. That is more than twice the impact of smoking marijuana, according to researchers. In *The Myth of Multitasking: How Doing It All Gets Nothing Done*,[6:5] Dave Crenshaw explains that switchtasking only serves to shorten our attention spans and make us more susceptible to interruptions – both internal and external. Interruptions and switchtasking create the self-induced ADD described above. When we try to focus on more than one thing at a time, we lose our ability to focus on anything. Reduce the amount of switchtasking you do each day.

## INTERVAL TRAINING FOR YOUR BRAIN.

If you were planning to run your first marathon, you wouldn't get up on the day of the marathon and expect to run 26.2 miles. So, if you're not accustomed to focusing for long periods of time, don't sit at your desk and tell yourself you're going to work for an hour or more on a project. It is a recipe for frustration. If you were training for a marathon, you'd start small and work up to 26.2 miles over time. My friends who have trained for marathons have all followed some type of interval training method. One of the best ways to condition your body is to use interval training. Our muscles respond very well to short bursts of intense training, followed by lighter training or rest. Our brains work the same way. You can increase your ability to focus by starting out with short blocks of focus time and building up to longer periods of intense focus. Here's how:

*   Get a timer for your computer. I use Egg Timer Plus by Sardine Software. I like it because it allows you to create custom timer presets.
*   Start small. Create a "Focus Preset" for 10 minutes and a "Break Preset" for two minutes. Tell yourself you are going to focus on a particular task, completely uninterrupted for 10 minutes. Then give yourself a two-minute break.
*   Create additional presets of 15 minutes, 25 minutes, 45 minutes, 60 minutes and 90 minutes. And create a five-minute break and a 10-minute break. You could also apply the concept of working 25 minutes and then taking a five-minute break. This way of working is known as The Pomodoro Technique. It's a powerful tool for getting work done in a highly focused way. For more information on The Pomodoro Technique, visit http://www.pomodorotechnique.com.
*   If you can, work up to 90 minutes of focus time. Then give yourself a 10-minute break. Brain research has shown that 90 minutes is the optimal amount of time our brains can focus on one thing.

## GET REGULAR EXERCISE.

Exercise is good for you. You already know that. But what you may not know is that exercise is not only good for your physical health; it's good for your brain. Regular exercise can help to improve your mental focus and dexterity. Even 15 minutes a day of aerobic exercise – something as simple as a brisk walk – can improve your ability to focus.

## GET ENOUGH SLEEP.

Most of us need at least seven to eight hours of sleep to be at our best. Recent research has shown that some people may need as many as nine hours a night.[6:4] Unfortunately, many of us suffer from "sleep debt," a chronic lack of sleep that can accumulate over time. Sleep debt not only impacts our ability to focus, it can lead to serious health issues such as increased risk of stroke, heart disease, weight gain, diabetes and memory loss.

## LIVING THE LESSON

* Notice when you are multitasking, and make a conscious effort to reduce the amount of multitasking you do each day.
* Turn off email notifications. Pop-ups and audio notifications are constant sources of distraction and can destroy your focus. Remember: If you're waiting for an important email, you can always check for it.
* Start with shorter periods for focus and work up to longer periods, but no longer than 90 minutes without a break.
* Try using earplugs to block extraneous noises. I got in the habit of using earplugs when I was studying for the bar exam. They can really help you shut out the world around you when you want to focus. You may also want to try listening to music with headphones to drown out distractions. The key to using music to help you focus is to find the right "background" music for you. You want the music to help you focus and not be a further distraction for you!

[6:1] Symptoms or criteria for diagnosis of ADD from the DSM-IV Diagnostic and Statistical Manual of Mental Disorders. Retrieved from http://www.mental-health-today.com/add/dsm.htm

[6:2] Hallowell, Edward M. (2007). *CrazyBusy.* Ballantine Books.

[6:3] Retrieved from http://blogs.hbr.org/hmu/2009/01/pay-attention-an-interview-wit.html.

[6:4] Jackson, Maggie (2009). *The Dangers of Distraction, The Erosion of Attention and the Coming Dark Age.* Prometheus Books.

[6:5] Crenshaw, Dave (2008). *The Myth of Multitasking: How Doing It All Gets Nothing Done.* Jossey-Bass.

*Lesson 7*

● ● ● ●

# GET IN THE HABIT OF PLANNING!

*To be prepared is half the victory.*

— MIGUEL DE CERVANTES

One of the most powerful things you can do to begin to take control of your time, your work, and ultimately your life, is to get into the habit of planning. The power of planning comes not from flawlessly executing your plans; that may rarely happen! Rather, the power comes from the planning itself.

As the German writer and philosopher Johann Wolfgang von Goethe (1749-1832) said, "Things which matter most must never be at the mercy of things which matter least." Planning is the means by which you can identify the "things which matter most." Without identifying "the things which matter most," you will constantly be reacting to things that are important to others. You'll always be putting out fires. Planning is the first proactive key to your time management success.

"But I'm too busy to spend time planning," I hear you thinking. Get that thought out of your head. The return on your investment of time spent planning has been estimated as high as three-to-one. That means that 30 minutes invested in planning this week may recoup you as much as 90 minutes next week.

Here's another reason why planning is so essential to your success. In his book, *The Way We're Working Isn't Working,*[7:1] Tony Schwartz talks about the concept of "predeciding." The concept of predeciding is a powerful way to change behavior. For example, if you want to stop eating junky, sugar-filled snacks at work, keep an assortment of healthy snacks in your desk drawer. By doing so, you've helped your brain "predecide" what you're going snack on, lessening your need to rely on willpower alone. Planning is just another way of predeciding. Rather than constantly reacting to other people's priorities, planning allows you to decide – in advance – how you will spend your day.

> Predeciding should help a person protect goal pursuit from tempting distractions, bad habits, or competing goals...When you go into a day that's unplanned, then you're just faced with whatever hits you. If you have a plan, then you don't let the unplanned things get in your way.
> – From *The Way We're Working Isn't Working*

You may not always be able to execute your plans flawlessly. But that's okay. As the old military saying goes: No plan survives contact with the enemy. And in your office, the enemy can appear in a variety of ways. Clients, opposing counsel, even the people on your team – sometimes it can feel like they're all out to thwart your best laid plans. The enemy is anyone or anything that blows up your plan for the day or the week. Yet, the truth is, the only way to be ready for the enemy is to plan. Remember, it is the act of planning itself that is powerful. Planning forces you to:

* Identify critical issues and deadlines
* Anticipate potential roadblocks
* Prioritize your work and focus on "what matters most"

## LIVING THE LESSON
**Take 30 minutes to plan your week.**

* Schedule a weekly appointment with yourself to do your weekly planning. I suggest a minimum of 30 minutes on Thursday or Friday to plan the coming week.
* Include your key support person in your planning session.
* During your planning session, look at your calendar for the next month. Make note of deadlines and due dates.
* Schedule time in your calendar during the coming week to actually do the work associated with those deadlines and due dates. (*See* Lesson 12. Schedule time to do your legal work *and* work on your goals.)

**Take 10 minutes at the end of the day to plan the following day.**

* Do this *before* your legal assistant or paralegal leaves for the day. I recommend building in a quick huddle at around 3:30 p.m. or 4:00 p.m. (*See* Lesson 10. Put an end to "lurk and blurt" with huddles.)
* Review your calendar for the next day. Do you have everything you need for the day? Are the files you plan to work on in your office or accessible on your desktop or tablet? Are you prepared for your hearing? Depo? Client meeting?
* Identify the one thing that you must accomplish tomorrow if everything else goes south!
* Make sure your key people are clear on their top priorities, as well.

**Use these focus statements with your team:**
If we do nothing else tomorrow, we must _____.
The single most important thing we must do this week is _____.

*You've got to think about the big things while you're doing small things, so that all the small things go in the right direction.*

— ALVIN TOFFLER

[7:1] Schwartz, Tony and Gomes, Jean (2010). *The Way We're Working Isn't Working.* Simon & Schuster, Inc.

## Lesson 8

● ● ● ●

# FOCUS ON DOING THE RIGHT THINGS.

*Every passing minute is another chance to turn it all around.*

— Cameron Crowe

Your ability to create powerful habits and use them to focus your attention on doing the right things will make a tremendous impact on your life. Throughout the day you're faced with choices about how to spend your time. The choices you make in each moment will either move you toward your goals or get in your way. They will either increase your sense of control and decrease your stress, or they won't. The choices you make each day about how you spend your time are creating your future. Right now.

In his book *Goals! How to Get Everything You Want – Faster Than You Ever Thought Possible*, [8:1] Brian Tracy shares what he describes as the most important question of all when it comes to time management: "What is the most valuable use of my time, right now?" I love this question. It forces you to evaluate what you're doing in the moment. It forces you to focus and prioritize.

But I'd suggest tweaking it just a bit. Instead of asking, "What is the most valuable use of my time, right now?" ask yourself, "Is what I'm doing right now part of my plan *and* moving me toward my goals?" This question gets

you in the habit of evaluating what you're doing on
the day or week, and your longer-term goals. It wi
moving in the right direction.

The issue isn't whether we get knocked off track.
track. The issue is how quickly we get back on track. A
York to Los Angeles will be off track over 90 percent _. ⊥ne pilots
(or onboard computers) constantly check the plane's instruments and make
course corrections that ultimately get them – and their passengers – to their
destination. Think of the question – "Is what I'm doing right now part of my
plan *and* moving me toward my goals?" – as your course correction during
the day.

## LIVING THE LESSON

* Get in the habit of asking yourself this question throughout the day:
  "Is what I'm doing right now part of my plan *and* moving me toward
  my goals?"

* Write this question on a sticky note and put it on your computer
  monitor, or anywhere you can see it. Keep it in front of you all the
  time.

* Ask the question, listen to the answer. Then, if necessary, make a
  course correction.

[8:1] Tracy, Brian (2010). *Goals! How to Get Everything You Want – Faster
Than You Ever Thought Possible.* Berrett-Koehler Publishers.

*Lesson 9*

●　●　●　●

# LEARN TO MANAGE NEEDLESS INTERRUPTIONS OR YOU'LL NEVER BE ABLE TO FOCUS ON ANYTHING.

*Sleep, riches, and health, to be truly
enjoyed, must be interrupted.*

— *Jean Paul Richter*

**U**nfortunately, what can be said of sleep, riches and health cannot be said of your work. Interruptions in the office serve only to increase your stress and decrease your effectiveness. How often do you come to the office in the morning, work like crazy all day, and then as you're getting ready to leave, stare at your "to do" list and think to yourself, "What did I do today?" If you have more days like this than you'd like to admit, you're not alone. The average manager or knowledge worker is interrupted every eight minutes. Interruptions kill your productivity. They kill your team's productivity. They are like evil little monsters that steal your time and attention. And you are losing more time than you realize to these nasty creatures.

## THE COST OF INTERRUPTIONS.

According to recent research, it can take the brain up to 20 minutes to recover from an interruption. So, if you're dealing with only three needless interruptions during your day, you're losing one hour. Over the course of a year, that adds up to around 240 hours or six, 40-hour weeks. Ouch! Do you bill by the hour? Do that math over the course of a year. Or, how about losing six weeks each year that you could be spending with your loved ones, golfing, biking, or relaxing on the beach? You get the idea.

Another insidious cost of interruptions: The work that gets interrupted often turns into the fire that needs to be put out down the road. A study by Microsoft showed that 40 percent of the time, work that was interrupted wasn't resumed after the interruption. Moreover, participants in the study reported that the more complex the interrupted task was, the more difficult it was to return to the task after the interruption.[9:1]

Think about how this research applies to your work as a lawyer. Constant interruptions can create a "time famine," the sense of having far more work to do than time enough to do it. But there is something you can do to end (or at least lessen) the time famine. Learn to limit needless interruptions.

Before we go any further, let's talk about what I mean by needless interruptions. Needless interruptions are those interruptions that are not both urgent and important. For example, an urgent and important interruption might be a phone call from your client on the deal you're working to close by the end of the day or an email from opposing counsel about settling the case set for jury selection tomorrow. There are also non-work-related things that can be urgent and important, such as family emergencies. But the reality is that most of the interruptions you deal with during the day *are not* both urgent *and* important. They don't need your immediate attention and could be addressed at another time. Learn to recognize and eliminate – or at least reduce – needless interruptions, and your life will improve dramatically.

## LEARN TO RECOGNIZE INTERRUPTIONS – BOTH EXTERNAL AND INTERNAL.

### External

External interruptions come from anyone or anything other than you. Most external interruptions fall into one of three categories:

1) Personal: Personal interruptions involve someone physically interrupting you. It could be your paralegal walking into your office to ask you a question. Or it could be an associate knocking on your door to strategize about a case she's working on. Or it could be your partner who wants to chat about what you did over the weekend. In each of these examples, you are being interrupted for something that could likely be addressed at another time.

2) Phone calls: Many phone calls are needless interruptions. Unless the call is about something that is both urgent and important, it could be scheduled for another time.

3) Email: Email is perhaps the worst external interruption of them all. Email is always there, interrupting you every few minutes if you let it. It can be a huge distraction and productivity killer.

**Internal**

Internal interruptions are self-inflicted interruptions such as checking email as a way to distract you from what you're working on. "Wait!" I hear you thinking, "You just told me email was an external interruption!" Bad news: It's an internal interruption, too. Surfing the Web is another internal interruption. Internal interruptions can also be triggered by external stimuli – for example, overhearing a conversation outside your door while you're working on a project, or noticing a ringing phone while focused on other work. We also interrupt ourselves when we need a mental break.

## LIVING THE LESSON
### Step 1

*   **Notice where your interruptions are coming from.** The first step in eliminating needless interruptions is knowing where they are coming from. The best way to do this is to keep an interruption log. Keep a legal pad handy and note each time that you are interrupted during the day. Track the following:

o   Was the interruption external? If so, was it personal, a phone call or email?

o   Was the interruption internal? Describe it.

o   Was it a needless interruption, or was it truly urgent *and* important?

o   What time of the day did the interruption occur?

o   What was the length of the interruption?

o   Did you return to the work you were doing when you were interrupted?

Keep the log for three days. They don't have to be consecutive days, but three days will give you a good idea of how many needless interruptions you deal with on a regular basis. HINT: If by mid-morning on your first day of keeping this log you have writer's cramp from noting all of your interruptions, then you are dealing with too many needless interruptions. Continue to Step 2.

## Step 2

*   **Reduce External Interruptions:** With respect to personal interruptions, make it a habit to have regular huddles with your key people. (*See* Lesson 10. Put an end to "lurk and blurt" with huddles.) Schedule time to return phone calls and process email. (*See* Lesson 11. Learn to batch certain tasks.)

*   **Reduce Internal Interruptions:** The first key to reducing internal interruptions is to develop your ability to focus. (*See* Lesson 6. Understand and apply the power of focus.) The second key is to know yourself. If you kept an interruption log, you likely noticed patterns of self-interruption. For example, if around 3:00 p.m. every afternoon, you wander into the kitchen for something to drink, pay attention. Your body is telling you something: You need a break. Why not build break times into your schedule? (*See* Lesson 12. Schedule time to do your legal work *and* work on your goals.)

**Step 3**

* **Schedule Focus Time:** In addition to scheduling time to complete tasks such as returning phone calls and processing email, schedule focus time in your calendar to work on your highest level work. This is time when you won't be interrupted, unless it is a true emergency. (*See* Lesson 7. Get in the habit of planning!)
* **Team Focus Time:** Just as focus time is important for you, it is important to everyone on your team. Make sure that everyone on your team is provided with time during the day when they can work uninterrupted. This may take some calendar coordination within the team. For example, if you work with two paralegals, you wouldn't want both of them to schedule focus time at the same time. Take the time to figure out how best to structure focus time for everyone in your firm. It will be well worth the investment.

[9:1] Czerwinski, Mary; Horovitz, Eric; and White, Susan. *A Diary Study of Task Switching and Interruptions*. Microsoft Research. Retrieved from: http://research.microsoft.com/en-us/um/people/horvitz/taskdiary.pdf.

## ADDITIONAL RESOURCES

*Time Management for Attorneys: A Lawyer's Guide to Decreasing Stress, Eliminating Interruptions & Getting Home on Time*, by Mark Powers and Shawn McNalis.

*Lesson 10*

•   •   •   •

# PUT AN END TO "LURK AND BLURT" WITH HUDDLES.

*People who enjoy meetings should not be in charge of anything.*

— THOMAS SOWELL

The lurk and blurt syndrome is prevalent in nearly every law firm. I first heard the phrase "lurk and blurt" from Mark Powers and Shawn McNalis, my Atticus colleagues and the authors of *Time Management for Attorneys: A Lawyer's Guide to Decreasing Stress, Eliminating Interruptions & Getting Home on Time.*[1:1] I love this expression because it so perfectly depicts something every lawyer I know has suffered from at one time or another. Lurk and blurt is insidious because of its ability to rob attorneys and staff alike of time and focus. Here's what lurk and blurt looks like:

You are sitting at your desk speaking to an important client on the phone. Out of the corner of your eye you see your paralegal standing in your doorway. You don't look at her directly, but you know she's there… lurking. You continue the conversation with your client. A few minutes later, she catches your eye again, and you notice she has some type of document in her hand. Now you're distracted, but you don't make eye contact with her, and you continue your conversation. A few more minutes go by, and you notice she's still lurking. This time, you glance her way, and she mouths the words, "I – JUST – NEED – ONE – MINUTE," holding up her index finger to emphasize her point. You nod, and motion for her to wait there. A few moments later, you say goodbye to your client, but before you can jot down a single note about the phone call, she races into your office and blurts out a question about the document she has in her hand. You answer her question, have a short conversation, and move on to your next task, completely forgetting to make any notes about the phone call you just had with your client.

That's a typical lurk and blurt scenario, but the ol' lurk and blurt can work in other ways, too. How often have you stood over your assistant's desk, asked what he's doing, and told him to do something else? Or maybe you've been chased to your car or followed to the restroom because someone on your team had a question for you? Lurk and blurt is frustrating for everybody involved. It's frustrating for the lurkers because they feel that the only way to get your attention is by stalking you. And it's frustrating for you, because you have no control over when the lurk and blurt will occur. There is a better way.

## HUDDLE WITH YOUR TEAM EVERY DAY.

Get in the habit of huddling with your key people every day. A huddle is a short meeting (emphasis on short!) that gives everyone on your team the opportunity to provide a quick status report regarding what they are working on for the day. Huddles also give you the opportunity to re-prioritize work, if you need to. Finally, huddles give your team access to YOU. It is their time to ask you questions about the things they are working on.

Huddles are similar to the stand-up meetings created as part of the Agile software development process. Stand-up meetings are short: five to 10 minutes maximum. The meetings are designed to foster improved communication team-wide. How many times have you heard someone in your office say to a co-worker: "Oh, I didn't know you were working on that!"? The improved communication that huddles create will minimize those moments and help to ensure that nobody's dropping the ball. Other wonderful side benefits of huddles are improved teamwork and better morale.

You might choose to have one huddle in the morning and another in the afternoon. Or you might decide to meet with certain people in the morning and others in the afternoon. You and your team need to determine what works best for your office. The important thing is that you make huddles a habit – and keep them short. You may even want to use a simple kitchen timer to make sure you don't run over time. Wind it up; set it for 10 minutes; and when it rings, the huddle is over. You might not be able to cover everything you want to in each huddle as you begin to establish this habit, but resist the urge to lengthen huddles. Keep them short and sweet, and you'll train yourself to stay on track.

As I mentioned, you and your team need to decide the best time for huddles; whether you'll huddle in the morning or the afternoon or both; and who will participate in each huddle. You'll also want to agree on a format for your huddles. There's no "right" agenda; figure out what works for you. Here are some ground rules to get you started.

## HUDDLE RULES

* Schedule huddles for the same time(s) and place every day.
* Be prepared.
* Be on time.
* Be brief. (If someone has a complicated question or issue, set another time to discuss it.)

## EACH TEAM MEMBER ANSWERS THE FOLLOWING QUESTIONS:

* What are the top three things you're working on today?
* Are there any obstacles in your way?
* What questions have you brought to the huddle?

Making huddles a habit will make everyone in your office tremendously more productive.

## ASK YOUR TEAM TO BATCH THEIR QUESTIONS.

Huddles are not only a great forum for status updates on what people are working on; they are your team's guaranteed access to you. Rather than interrupting you every time they have a question, ask everyone to keep a list of their questions for you. Then, ask them to bring their questions to the huddle with the understanding that if their question is both urgent and important, they don't need to wait until the next huddle. But if it's not, they add it to their list for the next huddle and move on to their next task. And here's the twist: Ask them to bring you at least one suggested answer for every question. By bringing a suggested answer to the question, you're challenging them to think on their own. You'll find that very often, they'll have the right answer. And if they don't, no harm done – it's an opportunity for everybody to learn the right answer.

Asking your staff to batch their questions is one of the most valuable things you can do to begin to take control of your time and limit needless interruptions. It's also a wonderful way to educate and empower your team.

## LIVING THE LESSON

*   Meet with your team to create a framework for huddles. Each team has different needs, so ask the following questions:
    o   What time or times during the day should we huddle?
    o   Do we need more than one huddle each day?
    o   Do we need huddles with different teams?
*   Put huddles in the calendar. Treat them as you would any important appointment.
*   Designate someone as the huddle captain. The huddle captain's job is to make sure that huddles take place. Hint: You should not be the

huddle captain because you're likely the first person to say, "We don't need to meet today."

[10:1] Powers, Mark and McNalis, Shawn (2008). *Time Management for Attorneys: A Lawyer's Guide to Decreasing Stress, Eliminating Interruptions & Getting Home on Time.* Atticus Ink.

*Lesson 11*

● ● ● ●

## LEARN TO BATCH CERTAIN TASKS.

*Most people haven't realized how out of control
their head is when they get 300 emails a day.*

— DAVID ALLEN

Batching similar tasks is a simple way to reduce the amount of multitasking you do. I know you'll never be able to completely eliminate multitasking. But you need to be aware of how multitasking (or switchtasking) can destroy your ability to focus. When you are switching back and forth between tasks, you are teaching your brain that focus is unimportant. This is exactly what you do not want to be teaching your brain! As your brain loses the ability to focus, you lose effectiveness and efficiency. The result? – Lots of wasted time and frustration. You already know these results because you've experienced them. How many times have you ended the day feeling as though you've not accomplished a thing because you've tried to accomplish too many things?

Let's take a closer look at the dangers of switchtasking. In a study conducted by the Federal Aviation Administration and the University of Michigan, young people between the ages of 12 and 24 were forced to switch between tasks such as solving math problems or categorizing shapes.[11:1] The research showed that the subjects lost time for all types of tasks when they had to switch from one task to another. Moreover, the study's results were similar to the Microsoft research regarding interruptions cited in Lesson 9, which showed that the more complex the interrupted task was, the more difficult it was to return to the task. Time lost increased significantly when participants had to switch between complex tasks. And here's more bad news about switchtasking: As we get older, we get even slower when switchtasking. So the less you have to switch from one task to another throughout the day, the more you'll be able to get done. In fact, research has shown that you can increase your productivity by up to 40 percent by batching similar tasks.

If you're thinking, "Okay, I'm in. Let's start batching tasks," here's some good news: You're already doing it. While you might not be batching tasks at the office, you're batching tasks at home, whether you realize it or not. You don't run your dishwasher every time you have a dirty dish. You don't do the laundry every time you throw something in the hamper. Right? Why? Running the dishwasher or the washing machine for just one or two items wastes energy and resources. It requires the same time and energy as it does for a full load of dishes or clothes. Your brain isn't a washing machine, but you're using up precious mental resources by switching back and forth between tasks.

In your office, there are all kinds of tasks you can batch to help your brain work more productively:

* Processing email
* Reviewing snail mail
* Drafting documents
* Reviewing and revising draft documents
* Signing documents

I'm sure you can think of other tasks, but this list will get you started. Once you get in the habit of batching tasks, you'll begin to experience a type of flow state as you plow through your work. This type of flow feeds on itself, and I'm betting that by identifying just one or two areas where you can batch tasks, you'll be looking for other areas.

## BE READY FOR THE UNEXPECTED "GIFT OF TIME"

The next time an appointment gets canceled, or a hearing is continued at the last minute, or you're stuck waiting at an appointment away from the office, don't get upset. Instead, view the change in circumstances as a gift of time. Time you have to spend on other tasks – batched tasks. Be ready for this gift by always being prepared to use it.

In *Getting Things Done: The Art of Stress-Free Productivity*, [11:2] effectiveness expert David Allen recommends four criteria that will help you choose what to do when you receive a gift of time. He calls the model "Choosing Actions in the Moment," and it's a great way to decide what to do when you have just a few minutes at hand, regardless of whether or not you're in your office. The key to making the most of this time is to ALWAYS have work available to you – either physically with you or available in the cloud. Alternatively, have access to your "to do" list so that you can bang through it when you have an unexpected gift of time. Rather than getting upset when you're waiting for a hearing or your client is running late, use the time to work through batched tasks. But what if you have only a minute or two? Those brief gifts of time are the perfect opportunity to just take a few deep breaths and focus on...nothing. (*See* Lesson 34. You are a leader. Be mindful of that.)

Here are the four areas David Allen suggests considering when you're presented with an unexpected gift of time:

1. Context: There are some tasks that cannot be accomplished without physically being in your office. Other tasks can be done regardless of where you are.
2. Time available: Do you have the next 10 minutes available – or the next hour?
3. Energy available: How much energy do you have? Are you feeling energized and creative, or are you feeling drained?
4. Priority: What can you do in the time available that will have the highest payoff? If your energy level is low, your biggest payoff might be simply cleaning your desk.

## LIVING THE LESSON

* Identify those tasks you can batch. Examples include processing emails, returning phone calls, reviewing your mail and signing documents.
* Schedule blocks of time to focus on these batched tasks. These blocks of time don't have to be big. You'll be amazed at how much you can accomplish in just 10 or 15 minutes when you're doing similar tasks.
* Make sure these time blocks are in your calendar so that you'll know at a glance what you're doing and when – and so will your staff.

[11:1] Rubinstein, Joshua and Evans, Jeffrey (2001). *Is Multitasking More Efficient? Shifting Mental Gears Costs Time, Especially When Shifting to Less Familiar Tasks.* Retrieved from: http://www.umich.edu/~bcalab/articles/APAPressRelease2001.pdf
[11:2] Allen, David (2002). *Getting Things Done: The Art of Stress-Free Productivity.* Penguin Books.

## *Lesson 12*

● ● ● ●

# SCHEDULE TIME TO DO YOUR LEGAL WORK AND WORK ON YOUR GOALS.

*Time = Life. Therefore, waste your time and waste
your life, or master your time and master your life.*

— *ALAN LAKEIN*

In Lesson 6, we focused on focus. Creating uninterrupted time to focus on the things you need to do is essential to your success and your sanity. But creating focus time is just one step in improving your productivity and effectiveness. Once you've increased your ability to focus, you need to put that focus to work for you. The problem is that even if you're doing all the right things to improve your focus, you're often so busy that your focus can easily be lost. If you're not making the time to do the things you need to do – both with respect to your legal work and your goals – then the ability to focus is not going to help you. As crazy as it may sound, you need to schedule time to do your work.

Think about your calendar for a minute. Even better, look at your calendar right now. What do you see? I'm betting you see client appointments, telephone conferences, hearings, depositions, trials, meetings. But what about the "work" that precedes or follows everything that's filling up your calendar right now? Do you schedule time to actually *do* your legal work? And what about your goals? Do you schedule time to work on those, too? I know some lawyers whose calendars are so tightly packed they don't even allow for travel time to and from meetings, let alone time to think or make notes after a meeting.

In his book, *A Factory of One: Applying Lean Principles to Banish Waste and Improve Your Personal Performance*,[12:1] Daniel Markovitz talks about the concept of "living in the calendar." I love this phrase! This is exactly the approach I'm referring to. In order to actually "do" the things you need to do, you need to make time for them. The time will not magically appear. When you live in your calendar and schedule all of your work in your calendar, you begin to take control of your time.

Most of us don't "live in our calendars." We live in our inboxes. When you live in your inbox, you are constantly reacting. There is always something in that inbox that can pull you away from what you want (or need) to be working on. Get out of your inbox and into your calendar.

**Start thinking about scheduling your time on two levels.** First, you have to schedule time to do your substantive work. Second, you need to schedule time to work on goals you've set or big picture things you want to accomplish. In the book *The 4 Disciplines of Execution*,[12:2] the authors describe our daily job as a whirlwind. I think most lawyers can identify with this analogy. All too often, lawyers get caught up in the whirlwind that is the practice of law. The whirlwind consists of those real emergencies and fires you have to put out. The whirlwind acts on you. For you to be able to get your substantive work done and work on your goals, you have to act on the whirlwind. These lessons offer strategies to lessen the swirl of the whirlwind – such as limiting interruptions, daily and weekly planning, and increasing your ability to focus. But the truth is, the whirlwind will always be there trying to suck you in. You cannot eliminate it; but you can lessen its power.

**Schedule time to do your legal work.** We talked about this in Lesson 7. Get in the habit of planning. You need to get in the habit of planning so that you can know what needs to be done and schedule time in your calendar to do your substantive work.

**Schedule time to work on your goals.** The challenge of goals – and whether or not we achieve them – comes down to actually doing the things we need to do on a daily basis in order to accomplish them. There is a saying about writing: *Don't sit down to write a book. Sit down to write a page.* Big goals are accomplished one step at a time – one task at a time. Schedule time to do the small things that make the big things a reality.

## LIVING THE LESSON

* **Get organized.**

   Getting organized is what Joseph Ferrari, author *of Still Procrastinating? The No Regrets Guide to Getting it Done,*[12:3] refers to as "your secret weapon in task completion." According to Ferrari: "You can and must have control over the elements in your environment that cause you to procrastinate." Paradoxically, *if* those piles of files around your office were actually reminding you to work on them, they wouldn't be there! Instead, those piles of files are helping you procrastinate by reminding you that you're going to work on them…tomorrow…or maybe next week. So, clean up your office and enlist the help of your staff to keep it organized. If you need help getting organized read *Getting Things Done*, by David Allen and visit his website at www.davidco.com.

* **Put all of your action items into one list.**

   Most lawyers are familiar with "To-do" lists. In fact, many lawyers have more than one "To-do" list – they maintain many lists simultaneously. There are tasks connected to substantive work; tasks connected to marketing; and tasks connected to office administration. Sometimes, lists are kept electronically – in a spreadsheet or in Outlook or in a case management program. All too often, there are so many tasks on to-do lists that the idea of doing those tasks becomes overwhelming and debilitating. Again, *Getting Things Done* is a great resource in helping you organize this information.

\*   **Live in your calendar.**

Schedule time to do your work and work on your goals. If you spend your days in back-to-back appointments, meetings and phone calls, you will never have the time to actually do the work you need to do. CAVEAT: Don't schedule every moment of your day. You need unscheduled time to allow for the unexpected. And don't forget to build in break time for yourself! Your brain needs breaks throughout the day to be at its best. Build those breaks into your new home – your calendar.

[12:1] Markovitz, Daniel (2011). *A Factory of One: Applying Lean Principles to Banish Waste and Improve Your Personal Performance.* CRC Press.

[12:2] McChesney, Chris, Covey, Sean, and Huling, Jim (2012). *The 4 Disciplines of Execution: Achieving Your Wildly Important Goals.* Simon & Schuster.

[12:3] Ferrari, Joseph R. (2010). *Still Procrastinating: The No Regrets Guide to Getting It Done.* John Wiley & Sons, Inc.

*Lesson 13*

●  ●  ●  ●

# DO THE HARDER THING FIRST.

*Never put off till tomorrow, what you
can do the day after tomorrow.*

*— MARK TWAIN*

If that's your motto, you're not alone. Procrastination is a big part of
the lives of most lawyers. Virtually everyone has procrastinated about
something at some point. According to Joseph Ferrari, author of *Still
Procrastinating? The No Regrets Guide to Getting it Done,*[13:1] research indi-
cates that 80-95% of college students procrastinate. Some people have
made it a way of life. Approximately 75% of us consider ourselves procrastinators; 50% say they procrastinate consistently; and 15-20% of adults
are chronic procrastinators.

Think about your life and practice for a moment. Is your office full of piles
of files on your desk and on the floor? Are you regularly late for meetings?
Do you put work off until "the last minute" because you "work best under
pressure"? Do you have trouble gauging how long a project will take? Do you
consistently underestimate the amount of time it will take you to write a brief
or draft a contract? These characteristics are clear signs of procrastination.

Below are a few other characteristics of procrastination listed by Ferrari; the list is not exhaustive. How many are true for you?

* I am regularly late for meetings and appointments.
* I feel uncomfortable saying no to others when I'm asked to do something.
* I have lots of clutter around me and tend to be disorganized at work, at home, and in my life in general.
* It really is not my fault that I start and finish projects at the last minute, if at all; other people and other tasks that I have to do get in the way.
* I find it so hard to make decisions; I'm not a good decision maker.
* I know what I should be doing to meet deadlines, but I simply don't do it.
* It is so hard for me to just get started. It's easier if I don't even begin.
* It is difficult for me to organize things and then to get started, so I simply don't do it.
* I tend to focus on short-term, immediate pleasures, and I really don't think of or consider the long-term positive outcomes that would result from getting my tasks done.

Before we go any further, let's take a look at what procrastination is. The word "procrastination" is derived from the Latin "procrastinatus" – to put off until tomorrow. Dr. Piers Steel of the University of Calgary and author of the *Procrastination Equation: How to Stop Putting Things Off and Start Getting Stuff Done,*[13:2] defines procrastination as "to voluntarily delay an intended course of action despite expecting to be worse off for the delay." Steel's definition gets to the insidious nature of procrastination. When we procrastinate we know we'll be paying the price down the road, but we can't seem to stop ourselves – or should I say – start ourselves. And the procrastination itself tends to suck the energy right out of us. This concept is articulated perfectly by Rita Emmett, author of *The Procrastinator's Handbook,*[13:3] as Emmett's Law: The dread of doing a task uses up more time and energy than doing the task itself.

So, most of us procrastinate. We do it even though we know we'll be worse off for the delay. And while we're doing it, the act of procrastinating is sucking the life right out of us. While overcoming our habits around procrastination can be a lifelong process, there are some things you can do now – yes now – to make some real changes. Here are three.

*You may delay, but time will not, and*
*lost time is never found again.*

*— BENJAMIN FRANKLIN*

## WAYS TO BEAT PROCRASTINATION

**Increase your willpower.**

Procrastination is a learned behavior. It is a habit that can be broken. A powerful way to break the procrastination habit is to increase your willpower. The good news is that willpower is like a muscle. And the bad news is that willpower is like a muscle. Here's what I mean: Just like your muscles, your willpower gets "tired" with repeated use. And just like you can strengthen your muscles with exercise, there are things you can do to strengthen your willpower. By increasing your willpower, you can begin to break the procrastination habit.

In her book, *The Willpower Instinct: How Self-Control Works, Why It Matters, and What You Can Do To Get More of It,*[13:4] Kelly McGonigal, Ph.D., suggests a three-part "willpower-training regime."

* Strengthen your "I Won't Power," by committing to not do something you do regularly. For example, not swearing. (This one was *&*!# hard for me!) Or using your non-dominant hand to open doors.
* Strengthen your "I Will Power," by committing to do something every day that you don't already do, such as calling your mother, taking the stairs, or meditating for five minutes.

 *  Strengthen "Self-Monitoring," by formally tracking something you don't typically pay attention to. For example, what you spend each day, what you eat, or how much time you spend watching TV.

If you experiment with these willpower-training exercises, you'll see that you're actually creating new habits. The exercises ask you to make simple, small changes to your daily routine. And making simple, small changes is the best way to create a good habit or break a bad one.

**Do the harder thing.** You've probably heard of the saying, "Eat that frog!" It refers to the concept of doing your ugliest task first. Do it; get it out of the way; move on. Eating frogs (figuratively speaking, of course) is a great way to develop your brain's prefrontal cortex which increases your willpower. *The Willpower Instinct* explains it this way: "Every willpower challenge requires doing something difficult, whether it's walking away from temptation or *not* running away from a stressful situation. The more often you consciously choose to do the harder thing first, the more you build your 'willpower muscle,' and begin to banish procrastination."

## LEARN TO MEDITATE. AS LITTLE AS FIVE MINUTES A DAY CAN MAKE A DIFFERENCE.

Neuroscientists have discovered that when you ask the brain to meditate, it gets better not just at meditating, but at a wide range of self-control skills, including attention, focus, stress management, impulse control and self-awareness. People who meditate regularly aren't just better at these things. Over time, their brains become finely tuned willpower machines. Regular meditators have more gray matter in the prefrontal cortex, as well as regions of the brain that support self-awareness.

- From *The Willpower Instinct: How Self-Control Works, Why It Matters, and What You Can Do To Get More of It*

Meditating just five minutes a day can make a difference. If you can work up to 10 to 15 minutes a day, that's even better. The point is, you don't have to possess the focus of a Buddhist monk to benefit from meditation. In fact, as McGonigal points out in her book, "…being bad at meditation is good for self-control." Why? A wandering mind is perfectly normal during mediation. The more you notice your mind wandering during meditation and bring it back to what you were focusing on, the more likely you are to notice when your mind is wandering during the rest of the day.

As McGonigal notes in her book, "Meditation is not about getting rid of all your thoughts; it's learning not to get so lost in them that you forget what your goal is. Don't worry if your focus isn't perfect when meditating. Just practice coming back to the breath, again and again."

## LIVING THE LESSON
**Increase Your Willpower with Meditation.**

* Sit in your chair with your feet on the ground. Check your posture. Sit up straight and relaxed. Keep your hands in your lap or on your armrests.

* Focus your attention on your breath. Your eyes may be open or closed. With each breath in, say the word "inhale" silently to yourself; with each breath out say "exhale." Imagine the air moving in and out of your lungs. Imagine the air "breathing you" as you remain relaxed.

* Notice what you are feeling – how it feels to breathe. Notice the sensation of your feet on the floor, the texture of your chair. If your mind wanders, notice that, too. But don't get frustrated; just bring your attention back to your breath. Do this for five minutes, and work up to 10 or 15 minutes, if you can.

[13:1] Ferrari, Joseph R. (2010). *Still Procrastinating: The No Regrets Guide to Getting It Done.* John Wiley & Sons, Inc.

[13:2] Steel, Piers Ph.D. (2010). *The Procrastination Equation: How to Stop Putting Things Off and Start Getting Stuff Done.* HarperCollins.

[13:3] Emmett, Rita (2000). *The Procrastinator's Handbook: Mastering the Art of Doing It Now.* Walker & Company.

[13:4] McGonigal, Kelly Ph.D. (2013). *The Willpower Instinct: How Self-Control Works, Why It Matters, and What You Can Do To Get More of It.* Avery Trade.

# Lesson 14

● ● ● ●

## DO IT. DELEGATE IT. DEFER IT. DITCH IT.

*Simplicity boils down to two steps: Identify
the essential. Eliminate the rest.*

– LEO BABAUTA

**D**o it. Delegate it. Defer it. Ditch it. That four-step work processing rule is pretty simple. Very simple. But just because something is simple doesn't mean it is easy. In fact, rarely is anything that's really worthwhile in life easy… at least not at first. And you may find that, at first, this simple concept is not easy to apply to your work. Stick with it. If you make this lesson a habit, you'll see tremendous gains in your effectiveness *and* productivity.

In his book *Getting Things Done: The Art of Stress-Free Productivity,*[14:1] David Allen talks about the importance of the three Ds: Do it, Delegate it, or Defer it. To that list I would add a fourth D: Ditch it. You can apply the four Ds to all of your tasks, action items, and everything in your inboxes – both your physical inbox and your email inbox. Think of the four Ds as a mental flow chart for processing your work. Apply them to everything you do until they become a habit. Let's take a look at each of the four Ds individually.

**Do it.** "Do it" refers to work that you can do quickly. David Allen refers to this as the "Two-Minute Rule." If you can do something in two minutes or less, do it. If it's an email that takes you 30 seconds to read and then reply with a quick one or two sentences, do it! Don't say to yourself, "Okay, I'll come back to that later." If you do that, you'll waste precious time tracking and managing those emails. You'll be amazed at how much more productive you'll be if you just get in the habit of applying the Two-Minute Rule.

**Delegate it.** The ONLY way you move on to this step in the flow chart is if you determine that the action will take you longer than two minutes. If it will, then ask yourself whether or not you're the person who needs to do it. If you're not the person who needs to do it, then delegate it. The operative phrase in the preceding sentence is "needs to do it." Before you determine whether the task can and should be delegated, ask yourself this question: Must the task be done by a lawyer?

If your answer to this question is "No," then, the task should be delegated to your assistant or paralegal. If your answer to this question is "Yes," and you work with an associate, then consider delegating the task. If your answer to this question is "Yes," and you're a solo, then you need to move to step three and defer it to another time.

**Defer it.** So, if you can't complete a task in two minutes or less *and* you're the one who needs to do it, defer it to another time. For tasks that fall into this category, you need to schedule time to actually complete them. You can schedule time in your calendar in 30-minute blocks for simpler tasks, such as following up on emails and letters or returning phone calls. For more complex tasks, such as drafting a contract or a brief or reviewing client documents, schedule time in your calendar to perform that work as well. For these more complex tasks, include as part of your calendar entry exactly what you're going to do during the scheduled time. For example: 9:00 a.m. to 10:00 a.m.: Draft motion to dismiss on Smith file. Creating this type of specificity in your calendar helps you stay focused on exactly what you need to do. (*See* Lesson 12. Schedule time to do your legal work *and* work on your goals.)

**Ditch it**. Everything else falls into this category. As you work through your inboxes and to-do list, ask yourself, "Do I need to *do* anything with respect to this item?" If the answer is, "No," ditch it.

There is an old productivity adage that says, "Never touch a piece of paper more than once." Nowadays, that "piece of paper" is often an email in your inbox. How many times have you "touched" an email more than once? Regardless, of whether you are processing your to-do list, the inbox on your desk, or your email inbox, make the four Ds a habit.

## LIVING THE LESSON

As I mentioned above, this four-step method for processing your work is simple. So to begin living it, just begin doing it.

* **Do it.** If something will take you less than two minutes to do, do it. Immediately.
* **Delegate it.** If the task will take longer than two minutes, ask yourself this question: Must the task be done by a lawyer? If you don't need to do it *and* someone else can do it, then delegate it.
* **Defer it.** If a task will take longer than two minutes to complete *and* you are the person who needs to do it, defer it until a later time, *and* schedule time *to do it* in your calendar.
* **Ditch it.** If a task doesn't fit into any of the three categories above, you do not have to do it. Ditch it. Delete it. Trash it.

If you'd like to learn more about David Allen's methods for productivity, visit his website at www.davidco.com.

*It does not take much strength to do things, but it*
*requires a great deal of strength to decide what to do.*

*— ELBERT HUBBARD*

[14:1] Allen, David (2002). *Getting Things Done: The Art of Stress-Free Productivity.* Penguin Books.

*Lesson 15*

● ● ● ●

# BE SMART ABOUT DELEGATION.

*Why have great talent if you're not going to use it?*

– DIANE THOMPSON, CEO, CAMELOT GROUP

Truly successful people understand the fallacy of the old axiom, "If you want something done right, do it yourself." The reality is, you cannot do it all yourself. Everyone has limits. Accept this reality and learn to delegate effectively.

Why do so many lawyers have trouble delegating? There are many reasons: It's hard to let go. You fear the task won't be done correctly. You think the work won't be up to your standards (READ: No one can do anything as well as you can). I'm sure there are a host of other reasons you could add to this list. One of the reasons I believe that lawyers struggle with effective delegation is that they are "cursed with knowledge." In fact, we all suffer from the "Curse of Knowledge." In their book, *Made to Stick: Why Some Ideas Survive and Others Die,*[15:1] authors Chip Heath and Dan Heath define the Curse of Knowledge this way:

Once we know something, we find it hard to imagine what it was like not to know it. Our knowledge has "cursed" us. And it becomes difficult for us to share our knowledge with others, because we cannot readily re-create our listeners' state of mind.

With respect to effective delegation, the Curse of Knowledge can cause us to forget to list particular steps in a process because they are so second nature to us that we can't imagine someone else not "getting it." Has your secretary ever returned a project to you done incorrectly? Have you looked at it and thought, "I know I told her (or him) exactly how to do this. I'll just do it myself." If you've answered, "yes," to these questions there is good chance you were "cursed" by your knowledge and didn't provide the level of detail required for the person to carry out the task correctly. (This assumes that the person to whom you're delegating is competent and capable of completing the task.) If you've graduated from law school, passed the bar exam, and have practiced law for even a short period of time, you are cursed with knowledge that certain members of your team simply don't have. Remember that when you're delegating, and you'll be able to delegate much more effectively.

In their book, *Time Management for Attorneys: A Lawyer's Guide to Decreasing Stress, Eliminating Interruptions & Getting Home on Time,*[15:2] Mark Powers and Shawn McNalis recommend using SMART Rules for Delegation. SMART Rules require that every delegated task be:

**Specific:** If there is a high level of trust and this is a frequently delegated task, you can be less specific. But if this is the first time a task is delegated, and there is little experience or familiarity, you must be very specific about all the actions to be taken, possibly putting them into written form, depending on the complexity of the task. Remember the Curse of Knowledge. Be specific.

**Measurable:** Establish a definable intended outcome or outcomes. If possible, quantify the result or results. State this clearly and ask for it to be repeated back to check for accuracy.

**Accountable:** Select someone who will take ownership of the project or task. Set up a process for timely progress reports. Encourage questions and provide support. Delegation isn't dumping. In return for accountability, be sure the person has everything they need to produce the result you expect.

**Realistic:** Allow extra time for mistakes that are part of the initial learning curve – just make sure you have a way to catch them. Don't delegate something that isn't humanly possible to accomplish in a given time frame. How often have you underestimated the amount of time it will take you to do something? Be realistic in your expectations of others. Make sure you provide adequate resources to get the job done. If time is short, more assistance may be required.

**Timely:** State very clearly the date for completion, any checkpoint dates, and the impact of not meeting the deadline. Remember that the first time any task or project is undertaken, it will take longer to accomplish. Expect increased efficiency with repetition.

*What may be done at any time will be done at no time.*

— SCOTTISH PROVERB

## LIVING THE LESSON

* **Create a delegation mindset.** Begin looking for opportunities to delegate both substantive and administrative tasks. Consider delegation as one of the first steps in your workflow process (*See* Lesson 14. Do it. Delegate it. Defer it. Ditch it.)
* **Use S.M.A.R.T. Rules for Delegation**. Clearly communicate your expectations for delegated tasks and projects. And don't forget to continue to communicate throughout the process.
* **Offer support.** Make sure the person responsible has the tools and information needed. Make yourself available for questions. Remember, delegation does not mean dumping. Delegation is not abdication.

* **Resist the urge to micromanage.** If you micromanage your delegated tasks, then your team will never take ownership of them. They will never take complete responsibility. Micromanagement might seem easier in the short term, but in the long run it will undermine your effectiveness and your team's efficiency and success.

* **Understand that people will make mistakes.** Everybody makes mistakes. You should create a culture in your firm in which it's okay to make mistakes. That culture carries with it the responsibility to admit mistakes, learn from them, and not repeat them. There are very few mistakes – even in a law firm – that can't be remedied if they are discovered and corrected. Serious problems arise when people are afraid to admit their mistakes and, instead, try to hide them. You must also be willing to admit *your* mistakes, take responsibility for them, learn from them, and move on.

* **Finally, delegate to people's strengths.** This is true regardless of whether you are delegating substantive legal work or administrative tasks. Give your people an opportunity to shine by, as often as possible, delegating work they enjoy.

[15:1] Heath, Chip, and Heath, Dan (2007). *Made to Stick: Why Some Ideas Survive and Others Die.* Random House.

[15:2] Powers, Mark, and McNalis, Shawn (2008). *Time Management for Attorneys: A Lawyer's Guide to Decreasing Stress, Eliminating Interruptions & Getting Home on Time.* Atticus Ink.

*Lesson 16*

●　●　●　●

# GET READY FOR VACATION.

*There was nothing like a Saturday – unless it was the
Saturday leading up to the last week of school and
into summer vacation. That of, course, was all the
Saturdays of your life rolled into one big shiny ball.*

— NORA ROBERTS, *RISING TIDES*

Vacations are a wonderful thing. You know what happens when you're getting ready to go on vacation? You go into hyper-focus mode, right? You can plow through work like nobody's business. You focus on completing tasks that have been hanging around. You can get your inbox down to (almost) empty. – All with the focus of a Zen master. Why? Because there is a light at the end of the tunnel.

Most of the time, we're so far into the tunnel that we can't even imagine seeing the light at the other end. But when we're getting ready for vacation, we're willing to work hard because we know there is a reward on the other side. I'd venture to say we're more than just "willing" to work hard; we actually enjoy it. That sense of focused productivity and flow can be a reward in itself. And it can also come from simply having something to look forward to.

Having something to look forward to not only heightens your focus on the work in front of you, it can actually improve your overall health and well-being. Just the expectation of an enjoyable activity can heighten our mood and boost our productivity. A study reported in *The Happiness Advantage*[16:1] found that people who just thought about watching their favorite movie actually raised their endorphin levels by 27 percent. That's significant because endorphins are essential to your business success.

Endorphins are a morphine-like substance produced by our bodies that produce feelings of joy and overall well-being. They help us tolerate pain more effectively and can even calm us down when we're stressed out. Endorphins make us feel good, and when we feel good, we can focus more easily and accomplish more. And besides, feeling good just feels good. You may have read one of the many articles about how exercise boosts endorphin levels. The "runner's high" is a euphoric feeling experienced by runners or anyone engaged in periods of intense exercise, and that "high" is related directly to endorphins. A study by Dr. Henning Boecker at the University of Bonn[16:2] in 2008 found that the level of euphoria people feel correlates directly to the endorphins produced. According to Dr. Boecker, "The greater the euphoria the runners reported, the more endorphins in their brain[s]."[16:3]

So how can you get the equivalent of a runner's high when you're at work? Create the expectation of a happy experience. As the study cited in *The Happiness Advantage* notes, just thinking about a future enjoyable experience can boost your endorphins. I like to think about vacation. When we're getting ready for vacation, we're looking forward to something, we're feeling good, and we are very, very focused. So, if you want to increase your productivity and just plain feel better, spend more time in "getting ready for vacation" mode. Get yourself into that mode as often as you can. Make it a game. "If I can get my inbox down to 10 by the end of the day, I get to…" "When I complete the first draft of this contract, I get to…" After I've reviewed this expert deposition, I get to…" You get the idea. If you can get yourself into "vacation mode" more often by rewarding yourself with little things you love, you will be more focused and more productive day-to-day. And if you're more focused and more productive day-today, you really will be able to go on more vacations.

## LIVING THE LESSON

*   Build "vacation focus" into your workday.
*   Create "mini-vacations" or rewards for yourself, and work toward them during your day. Do you like to shop on Amazon or check sports scores or stocks online during the day? Then allow yourself breaks to surf the Web. But set goals around your Web surfing "vacation." For example, for every five "to-do's" you cross off your list, you allow yourself five minutes to surf the Web. Figure out what works for you!
*   You can also create "mini-vacations" that actually take you out of the office: an afternoon of golf, a massage, a bike ride, a manicure.
*   Set clear goals, and get in the habit of rewarding yourself for hitting them.
*   Make it fun! By rewarding yourself for increasing your ability to focus, you'll dramatically increase your productivity.

[16:1] Achor, Shawn (2010). *The Happiness Advantage: The Seven Principles of Positive Psychology That Fuel Success and Performance at Work*. Crown Business.
[16:2] Boecker, Dr. Henning (2008). *The Runner's High: Opioidergic Mechanisms in the Human Brain*. Retrieved from http://cercor.oxfordjournals. org/content/18/11/2523.long
[16:3] Kolata, Gina (2008). *Yes, Running Can Make You High*. Retrieved from http://www.nytimes.com/2008/03/27/health/nutrition/27best.html?_r=1&.

*Lesson 17*

● ● ● ●

## TAKE A BREAK, FOR CRYING OUT LOUD!

*Take a rest; a field that has rested gives a bountiful crop.*

*– OVID, 43 B.C. – 17 A.D.*

In a culture of – work hard, work late, work long, no matter what you are working on – the idea of taking breaks during the day may seem counterintuitive. The legal profession, perhaps more than any other, reveres the idea of working non-stop, ridiculously long hours. It's a badge of honor to be the last lawyer to leave the office at night. Some might say the culture is a product of the billable hour. That may be, but I know many lawyers who don't bill by the hour and who are stuck in the same pattern – lawyers who are still at their desks when their family is having dinner at home. They're doing that "just one more thing" that they didn't get to earlier in the day. Unfortunately, the lawyers stuck in this pattern are often the victims of their own best intentions. When you're working all day long without giving yourself breaks along the way, you're actually diminishing your effectiveness and productivity. And when you're not productive during the day, you'll end up staying late to get more done. And after all, isn't that what lawyers are expected to do? It's a vicious cycle.

If you want to break the cycle and be more productive *and* effective throughout the day, you must pay attention to another cycle. About every 90 minutes throughout the day, our bodies move from periods of higher alertness to lower alertness, in a pattern called the Ultradian Cycle.

> In effect, our bodies are asking us for a break every 90 minutes or so. More often than not, and especially in the face of high demand, we ignore signals such as physical restlessness, wandering attention and greater irritability. Instead, we grab a cup of coffee or unconsciously call up our emergency reserves, in the form of stress hormones such as adrenaline and cortisol. These hormones generate energy, but they also prompt a higher level of anxiety and reactivity, which ultimately undermine our effectiveness.
> - From *The Way We're Working Isn't Working*[17:1]

Although the Ultradian Cycle is our bodies' way of telling us that we need a break, most of us just don't listen. Instead of paying attention to these signals, we just keep going. When this happens, our bodies are being hijacked by stress hormones. While we might feel like we have a second wind, we're really being driven by what neuroscientist Robert K. Cooper calls "tense energy." In Cooper's book, *The Other 90% – How to Unlock Your Vast Untapped Potential for Leadership and Life*,[17:2] he explains how taking breaks during the day fulfills our bodies' need for rejuvenation.

Recent medical studies have underscored the importance of taking breaks throughout the day. In fact, getting up from your desk and taking a break may not only increase your mental clarity and boost your energy, it may improve your overall health and well-being. According to a study in the March 2012 issue of Archives of Internal Medicine and reported by CBS news:[17:3]

> [R]esearchers discovered that people who sat for 11 hours a day or more were 40 percent more likely to die – from any cause. The researchers also found the odds of dying were 15 percent higher for those who sit between eight to 11 hours a day compared to those who sit less than four hours a day.

In addition, research from the American Institute for Cancer Research found that that too much sitting increases the risk for colon cancer and breast cancer.[17:4] The same study stressed the importance of taking hourly breaks of one or two minutes. Those breaks can be something as simple as standing up and stretching or walking to the window.

In *The Other 90%*, Cooper suggests taking what he refers to as "strategic pauses" and "essential breaks" as a means to boost energy and mental clarity. A strategic pause is no more than 30 seconds, and it is taken every 30 minutes throughout the day. A strategic pause gives you the opportunity to breathe and stretch. An essential break is just a bit longer, two to three minutes, taken at least two times during the day. I would recommend taking an essential break every 90 minutes or so, in response to your body's own Ultradian Cycle.

Cooper suggests that the following components be part of any strategic pause or essential break:

* **Deepen and relax your breathing.** Focus on your breathing as you take 10 relaxed breaths.
* **Change your view.** Look out the window or at photos of loved ones. It's important to give your eyes a break from staring at the computer screen during the day.
* **Sip ice water.** The refreshing cold stimulates energy production and raises alertness. Research has also found that sipping ice water can help to burn calories throughout the day.
* **Get up and move!** Every time you get up and move or stretch, you receive an energy boost and achieve increased mental clarity. I keep a few free weights in my office so that when I take breaks, I can get in a few lifts!
* **Add some humor or inspiration.** Stop for a moment to recall a fond memory or watch a funny video on YouTube. You'll inject positivity into your day, which helps to boost your creative thinking.

## LIVING THE LESSON

* Make it a habit to take strategic pauses and essential breaks throughout the day.
* Schedule reminders on your computer or phone, to get in the habit of taking breaks during the day.
* Create one "meditation break" during the day. Sit in your chair with your feet on the floor, close your eyes and simply notice your breath. With each inhalation, say in your mind, "Inhale," and with each exhalation, "Exhale." Even a two-minute meditation break can have a powerful, positive effect on your ability to focus throughout the day.
* Make sure you stand up and stretch at least every 90 minutes! Every 30 minutes is even better.

*Most people live in a very restricted circle of their potential being. We all have reservoirs of energy and genius to draw upon of which we do not dream.*

*— WILLIAM JAMES*

[17:1] Schwartz, Tony (2010). *The Way We're Working Isn't Working.* Free Press.
[17:2] Cooper, Robert K. (2002). *The Other 90% - How to Unlock Your Vast Untapped Potential for Leadership and Life.* Crown Business.
[17:3] Castillo, Michelle (2012). *Sitting Too Much May Double Your Risk of Dying, Study Shows.* Retrieved from http://www.cbsnews.com/news/sitting-too-much-may-double-your-risk-of-dying-study-shows/
[17:4] *How Sitting and Moving Link to Cancer Risk* (2012). Retrieved from: http://preventcancer.aicr.org/site/News2?id=21401

# Lesson 18

● ● ● ●

## JUST HANGING YOUR SHINGLE AIN'T ENOUGH.

*Marketing takes a day to learn. Unfortunately,
it takes a lifetime to master.*

– PHILIP KOTLER

Once upon a time, if you were a good lawyer and did good work, you'd have all the clients you could handle. Your reputation was all that mattered. Your reputation was all you needed to build a successful law practice. Once upon a time, lawyers didn't need to think about marketing. There may have been a time when having a spotless reputation for excellent work was all it took to get clients knocking on your door. Those days are gone.

Yet, many lawyers still believe the fairy tale. In fact, law school might have even taught you that marketing was a dirty word. Oh, I know, your professors never actually talked about marketing being a dirty word. They probably never talked about marketing at all. Law schools – as the old saying goes – teach students how to "think like a lawyer." Unfortunately, they don't teach students how to think like a business person. Consequently, too many lawyers don't know how to succeed in the profession. The very things you need to know about creating a successful practice are simply not taught in law school.

While doing excellent substantive work can help you build your practice, it takes much more than just great work to sustain a thriving and successful practice. You must be able to effectively market your practice.

What do I mean by "effectively market your practice"? When I speak of marketing in these 50 Lessons, I'm talking about building relationships. It's all about the relationship. Whether face-to-face or online, it's all about the relationship. It's about you and how you connect with people. Being a great lawyer is just the first step in building a great practice. To build a great law practice, you must become a great marketer.

In, *Selling the Invisible*,[18:1] author Harry Beckwith explains that, "Marketing is not a department. It is your business." It is everything about your business. (*See* Lesson 21. Marketing – it's not just for partners anymore. Everything is marketing.) If you're uncomfortable with the idea of marketing, I have three words for you: Get over it. You can become a great marketer. You must become a great marketer. The good news is that marketing is a skill that can be mastered. There are an infinite number of ways that you can market your practice by simply doing what you love. (*See* Lesson 33. Hate marketing? Do what you love.)

The first step to becoming a great marketer is to simply let go of the fairy tale. Understand that marketing is a skill you can master – just like you mastered civil procedure or contracts or constitutional law. You can do this.

If the idea of marketing makes you uncomfortable, that's okay. Growth can be uncomfortable. Change can be uncomfortable. Just get comfortable with being uncomfortable.

*Life begins at the end of your comfort zone.*

*– NEALE DONALD WALSCH*

If the idea of marketing scares you, then feel the fear and do it anyway. You've probably been uncomfortable and scared many times in your career. But you moved past those feelings to get where you are today. Successful people are willing to push through the fear to accomplish their goals. As you'll hear me say many times in these 50 Lessons, just take a small step.

Start by doing one thing. Just one thing every day. Small changes can make a huge impact over time.

And if you want to know the secret to building your marketing muscle right now, here it is: **You've got to focus on building relationships.** Those relationships are built first by being able to speak passionately about how you help people. (*See* Lesson 31. Perfect your pitch. Be authentic, engaging, and powerful.) You've also got to build and nurture a robust and professional Internet presence that supports and enhances the personal relationships you create. (*See* Lesson 27. Marketing is about creating and nurturing real relationships. It's that simple.) And you've got to have a plan that keeps your marketing efforts on track. (*See* Lesson 22. Make time for marketing, even when you're busy.) And remember – you've got to build relationships. You've got to build relationships. You've got to build relationships.

> *The purest treasure mortal times can*
> *afford is a spotless reputation.*
>
> – WILLIAM SHAKESPEARE

## LIVING THE LESSON

* Get comfortable with the idea of marketing.
* Commit to learning all you can about how to effectively market yourself and your law firm.
* Join a Toastmaster's group in your area to improve your public speaking skills.
* Find ways to market your practice that are fun for you. (*See* Lesson 33. Hate marketing? Do what you love.)

[18:1] Beckwith, Harry (1999). *Selling the Invisible: A Field Guide to Modern Marketing.* Hachette Book Group.

## ADDITIONAL RESOURCES

*What Clients Love*, by Harry Beckwith.

*Quiet: The Power of Introverts in a World that Won't Stop Talking*, by Susan Cain.

*Feel the Fear and Do It Anyway*, by Susan Jeffers.

## Lesson 19

● ● ● ●

## CREATE A GREAT BRAND.

*A brand is a person's gut feeling about a*
*product, service, or company.*

— *Marty Neumeier, ZAG: The #1 Strategy*
*of High-Performance Brands*

Does your law firm have a brand? The answer is yes. The answer is yes, whether or not you've ever given one moment's thought to the idea of branding. The answer is yes, even though you may not know your brand even exists, or what defines it at its core. The answer is yes, although what you think your brand is might not be your brand at all.

Confusing? Not really. Stick with me. So, what exactly is a brand? Marty Neumeier's definition at the beginning of this lesson gets to the heart – or should I say guts – of the matter. Here's the thing: Your brand is not your logo. It is not your website. It is not your stationery or firm brochure. All those things are a part of your brand, but they are only a part.

Here's the truth: Your brand is how you are perceived by others. That's it. Your brand is perception – and perception is reality. Or in this case perception is your brand. Your brand is not what you say it is; your brand is what your clients say it is. Your brand is what your team says it is. How people feel about you, what your clients say about you and your firm, what you team says about you and your firm – these things create and nurture your brand. Your brand is how you make people feel. And how you make people feel essentially defines you and your firm.

> People create brands to bring order out of clutter. If the word BRAND didn't exist, we'd have to invent a new one, because no other word captures the complexity and richness of this concept. The only word that comes close is "reputation." Your personal reputation, like a company's brand, lies outside your control. It's not what YOU say it is— it's what THEY say it is. The best you can do is influence it.
> - From *ZAG: The #1 Strategy of High-Performance Brands* [19:1]

## THREE STEPS TO BUILDING A GREAT BRAND.

Your brand is EVERYTHING about your firm. Your logo, website, stationary and firm brochure are part of your brand, but they are just a part. Your brand is…How promptly you return phone calls…How welcoming, neat, and tidy your office (yes, YOUR office) is…How your receptionist answers the phone…How prepared you are for meetings or hearings…How you speak to clients…How your legal assistant speaks to clients…What your reception area looks like…Whether your shoes are shined…Whether your car is clean… Whether you deliver projects on time. You get the idea. Your brand is everything. Everything. Everything.

Although you can't create a brand by fiat, you can influence how people feel about you and your firm. You can influence your brand in everything you do. Start by thinking about branding your firm as a three-step process.

### 1. Know who you are, what you do, and what makes you "the only."

Before you can influence your brand, you have to know what you want to convey. The first step in building your brand is to get very clear about who you are and what you do. What is your mission? What is your law firm's mission? What do you stand for? Who are your ideal clients? How do you help them? Why do your best clients hire you? What makes you unique? Or in

Marty Neumeier's words: "What makes you the only?" If you can't answer these questions, you cannot build a brand.

**2. Spread the word.**
Now that you know your mission, who your ideal clients are and what makes you unique, you must let the world know. This is where your logo, your Internet presence (including your website, LinkedIn and Facebook profiles, YouTube videos, and all other social media) and all your other marketing materials come in. Your firm's image and message on the Web and across all of your marketing materials must have a consistent look and feel. But spreading the word goes far beyond your marketing materials. Remember, your brand is EVERYTHING. Your brand must be conveyed in everything about your firm. You must "live" your brand every day.

**3. Live it.**
Your job in building, or influencing, your brand is to create your brand experience in every aspect of your practice – and your life. Living your brand provides the greatest opportunity to influence the perception of your brand. Do you return your calls when you say you will? Does your office create an experience that is consistent with what you want to convey, or is it a mess, with files scattered all over the place? When people walk into your office, is it welcoming? When you go to a bar association luncheon, are your shoes shined? Is your purse overflowing with everything from yesterday's lunch wrapper to crumpled tissues? When a client calls your office, are they greeted warmly, or do they feel like they're just another problem to deal with? Are you likeable? Are you trustworthy?

If you live your brand, you'll create a total brand experience, and your clients will feel good about you and your firm. Then they'll spread the word for you.

## A TRUE STORY
When I was a kid, my dad started every joke he told – and he told some good ones – with, "And this is a true story." I don't think my dad ever meant those words, but I do. This is a true story.

A few years ago, a friend of mine stopped me at the state bar convention to tell me about his brother. His brother is a prominent pediatrician in their city, and he had been grocery shopping on a recent weekend. After my friend's brother loaded his groceries into his car, he walked his shopping cart to the cart corral rather than just leaving it in the parking lot where it could roll into someone's parked car. A woman and her three kids were nearby, and she watched him as he walked back to his car. She walked up to him and told him how thoughtful he was to have put his shopping cart away where it couldn't damage other cars. He thanked her, and they struck up a conversation. At the end of the conversation, my friend's brother had three new patients – the woman's children. Everything you do influences your brand. Everything.

## LIVING THE LESSON

* Set aside some time to really think about what you want your brand to be.
* Here are some questions to get you started:
  o What is your firm's mission?
  o What do you stand for?
  o Who are your ideal clients?
  o Why do they hire you?
  o How do you help them?
  o What makes you unique?
* Make sure everything about your firm is consistent with how you want your brand to be perceived. Remember, you can only influence your brand. Your clients, your team, and everyone you interact with define what your brand is.
* Know that everything you do matters. Everything you do influences your brand. (*See* Lesson 39. Words matter. They create your life.)

[19:1] Neumeier, Marty (2006). *ZAG: The #1 Strategy of High-Performance Brands*. New Riders.

## ADDITIONAL RESOURCES

*You are a Brand!: In Person and Online, How Smart People Brand Themselves for Business Success*, by Catherine Kaputa.

*The Brand Mindset: Five Essential Strategies for Building Brand Advantage Throughout Your Company*, by Duane Knapp.

*Build a Brand in 30 Days, With Simon Middleton, The Brand Strategy Guru*, by Simon Middleton.

*Engage! The Complete Guide for Brands and Businesses to Build, Cultivate and Measure Success in the New Web*, by Brian Solis.

*Lesson 20*

●　　●　　●　　●

# THINK OF MARKETING LIKE BRUSHING YOUR TEETH. DO IT EVERY DAY.

*Motivation is what gets you started.*
*Habit is what keeps you going.*

— *JIM ROHN*

I know something about you. I know that one of the first things you do after you wake up in the morning is brush your teeth. Maybe you even floss. You brush your teeth without notes and reminders to help you remember to do it. You don't wake up in the morning and have a conversation with yourself about the merits of good dental hygiene. You just get up, pad into the bathroom and brush your teeth. It's part of your morning routine. Here's another thing I know about you: After you brush your teeth, you don't say to yourself, "Whew, that's done! Don't have to worry about that for another month." Nope. You do it every single day.

I want you to start thinking of marketing like brushing your teeth. Marketing should be something you do every single day. Marketing isn't something to be done once a month or even once a week. You don't brush your teeth just once a month or once a week. You brush your teeth every day, twice a day, maybe three times a day. Just like brushing your teeth, you've got to make marketing part of your day – every day. If you want your law practice to thrive and grow, you can't go to a luncheon or cocktail party and say to yourself, "Okay, I've done my marketing for the month." Nope. You've got to do a little marketing every day. Make a phone call. Send an email. Post a status update on LinkedIn. Write a note. Go to lunch. Have a beer with a friend. Play a game of golf. Go shopping. Yes, these are all things you can do to market your practice. (*See* Lesson 33. Hate marketing? Do what you love.)

Here's why I want you to think of marketing like brushing your teeth: Brushing your teeth is a habit – a good habit. You don't think about brushing your teeth. You just do it. I want you to make marketing a habit.

Making marketing a habit is as simple as doing just one thing each day. Do just one thing, every day. It's the "every day" part that's important. Consistency is key when you're creating a new habit. (*See* Lesson 5. Create 12 new GOOD habits each year.) And remember: Small, incremental changes can have a huge impact over time. Don't worry that you're not doing enough. Start small by doing just one thing each day. You will be amazed at how doing just one thing will begin to change how you feel about marketing.

When you make marketing a habit, you'll create a marketing mindset that allows you to see marketing opportunities everywhere. One of my clients told me that she'd been approached by a partner from a large business law firm. She has a small, successful practice. She's worked in big firms before and has no desire to go back. She told me that her "old self" would have said, "No, thank you," and that would have been the end of the conversation. But her "new self" – the one with the marketing mindset, told that partner, "I truly appreciate the offer, but I want to keep my own firm. I'd love to have lunch and find out how we could each help each other, though." "I never used to think that way," she told me, "But now, I'm always looking for ways to market my practice."

Marketing opportunities are everywhere. When you make marketing a habit, you'll begin to look for marketing opportunities everywhere. And you'll find them!

## LIVING THE LESSON

* Do at least one thing each day to market your practice. Send an email to a friend. Call a client just to check in. (I guarantee that they will be bowled over.) Send a note to a colleague mentioned in your local bar association newsletter or state bar news. Until your "one thing" becomes a habit, put reminders in your calendar and ask one of your colleagues to be your accountability partner.

* Develop a marketing mindset. Always be on the lookout for ways you can help other professionals market their practices. As the old saying goes, "The best way to get a referral, is to give a referral." In the words of Tim Sanders, author of *Love is the Killer App,*[20:1] be a "love-cat." Tim's book was written in 2002, but its wisdom about connecting in the new economy still resonates with me. Lovecats help others by sharing knowledge, connecting people and showing compassion. Develop your marketing mindset with a dash of lovecat thinking.

* Look for situations in which you can ask yourself: "How can this benefit my practice?" "Can I turn this situation into an opportunity to connect with a new person?" "Is there some way I could be of service in this situation?" "Can I share knowledge?" "Can I make an introduction?" "How can I help?"

[20:1] Sanders, Tim (2003). *Love is the Killer App.* Crown Business.

## ADDITIONAL RESOURCES

*Never Eat Alone: And Other Secrets to Success. One Relationship at a Time*, by Keith Ferrazzi.

*Lesson 21*

●　　●　　●　　●

# MARKETING – IT'S NOT JUST FOR PARTNERS ANYMORE. EVERYTHING IS MARKETING.

*There are no magic wands, no hidden tricks and no secret handshakes that can bring you immediate success, but with time, energy, and determination, you can get there.*

— *Darren Rowse*

There was a time when the thinking among virtually all law firms was that partners were rainmakers. Partners were responsible for marketing the firm. Partners were responsible for finding new clients and bringing in the work. Associates were responsible for doing the work. Period. Associates weren't encouraged to market the firm. Oh, they may have been encouraged to join their local bar association or civic organization and asked (translation: required) to attend their meetings. But it usually stopped there.

Unfortunately, too many firms still embrace this dangerously outdated thinking. And those that do, do so at their own peril. In today's world, marketing is everyone's job. From partner to associate to paralegal to legal assistant to law clerk – everyone has a part to play in marketing the firm.

Firms that cling to the "Partners as Rainmakers" mentality simply won't survive in the 21st century. Partners, associates, and everyone on your team has a marketing role to play, and marketing contributions to make. Remember: Just as everything about your firm influences your brand (*See* Lesson 19. Create a great brand.), everything you do is marketing. Everything. Your receptionist is marketing every time she picks up your phone. Your paralegal is marketing when she calls a client to provide a case update. Your office manager is marketing when she designs (Yes. I said designs.) your invoices. You and your associates are marketing with every client interaction. You're marketing when you're in the office. You're marketing when you're out of the office. Whether you know it or not, you are marketing 24/7. Everything you do is marketing.

## PARTNERS

It's your responsibility to lead by example. As a leader in your firm, you set the tone for everything, including how everyone around you thinks about marketing. Make sure you're doing everything you can to market your practice and the firm. Partners should also serve as marketing mentors for associates. Just as you would mentor young lawyers in the substantive areas of your practice, be a marketing mentor for your associates. Give them opportunities to develop their marketing skills in order to help you grow the firm. Take them with you to lunches with clients and referral sources. Let them learn from your example how to create business for the firm. And if you're worrying that your associates will become great marketers and decide to leave you and start their own firm, that's a legitimate concern. But it's one you have to get over. (*See* Lesson 44. Money matters, but it's not the most important thing.) In order to build a successful law firm in the 21st century, everyone in the firm needs to find a way to market.

Create a marketing mindset for the entire firm. Let everyone know that every time they interact with someone, it's an opportunity to market the firm. Whether it's a potential client, current client, vendor, colleague or even opposing counsel, every interaction is an opportunity to market. A friend of mine who does defense work once told me that every time he called the office of one of the law firms he litigated against, he was so impressed with how he was treated that he referred an injured friend to them. Once you let everyone on your team know how important they are to marketing the firm, ask everyone on your team for their ideas on how you could improve client service. Ask them to ask themselves: "What is the one thing I could do to improve how we serve our clients?"

## ASSOCIATES

Step one is to learn as much as you can about marketing. You probably didn't learn much about marketing in law school, but there is a tremendous amount of information available in books and online. Not to mention the lessons in these 50 Lessons that are focused on marketing – specifically, Lessons 18 through 33.

Next, find a mentor – ideally a mentor within your own firm. But if you can't find a mentor in your firm, find one somewhere else. Learn everything you can from someone who is already doing it. You'll be amazed at how much you can learn from a marketing mentor.

Then, you've got to just do it! Get out there and put what you've learned to work for you. Focus on doing what you love. (*See* Lesson 33. Hate marketing? Do what you love.) Do you enjoy writing? Then write for your local bar association newsletter. Do you enjoy speaking? Volunteer to present at a CLE – or even better, create a presentation that you can take right to your client's office. Is there a charity that you're passionate about? Get involved. Maybe your firm would sponsor a fundraiser for it. Reach out. Make a commitment to contact at least three people each week – ideally in face-to-face meetings such as breakfast or lunch. If that doesn't work, pick up the phone. I think you'll be pleasantly surprised by how people react when you call them and simply ask how they are doing. I can guarantee that the conversation will strengthen the relationship.

## EVERYONE ELSE

Marketing is the engine that drives the success of the firm. EVERYONE in the firm can add fuel to the engine. Whether you are a partner leading a team of 50, or a sole practitioner working with a paralegal, make sure every person you work with knows the importance of their contribution to marketing the firm. Make it fun. The idea of marketing can be intimidating to even the most seasoned attorneys, but it doesn't have to be. Focus on creating and strengthening relationships with everyone who comes into contact with the firm – clients, potential clients, staff in other law firms, other lawyers, and yes, even opposing counsel. Marketing is about relationships. Real relationships. Build relationships and you will build your firm.

## LIVING THE LESSON

* Never stop learning about marketing. Set a goal to read at least one book on marketing each month. Or if that seems like a lofty goal, try listening to audiobooks. You can listen in your car, at the gym, or on walks, bike rides or runs. Make sure your reading (or listening) is not just about legal marketing. You can learn a lot from books on marketing that have nothing to do with legal marketing.

* Use online marketing resources. www.MarketingProfs.com offers some great content as part of its Basic (Free) membership, or you can pay for an annual membership which offers more. The Legal Marketing Association (www.legalmarketing.org) provides downloadable content geared specifically toward lawyers and law firms. If you want to jump-start your out-of-the-box marketing thinking, subscribe to Seth Godin's blog. He is brilliant.

* Plan a monthly marketing "Lunch and Learn" for your team. Ask each person to share an idea or one thing they've done to market the firm in the past month.

* Lead by example. Discover what you love and do it.

* Be consistent. Do at least three specific things each day to market your firm. By specific I mean, specifically focused on marketing and relationship building – make a phone call, send an email, write a blog post, share an update on one of your social media networks. You get the idea.

## Lesson 22

● ● ● ●

# MAKE TIME FOR MARKETING EVEN WHEN YOU'RE BUSY.

*Build a little community of those you love and who love you.*

MITCH ALBOM, TUESDAYS WITH MORRIE

If you're like many lawyers, your marketing efforts are dictated by how busy you are. The busier you are – the more clients or cases you have – the less you feel the need to market. Then, when things slow down because you haven't been consistently marketing the practice, you become intensely motivated to get out there and market. Sound familiar?

The problem with this pattern of on-again, off-again marketing is that it creates a crazy cycle of ups and downs – feast or famine. If you're not busy, you're marketing; if you are busy, you're not. When the work is right there in front of you, you're focused on the work and thinking to yourself, "I'm just too busy right now to be out there marketing. I'm a lawyer. I've got to get my work done." Yes, you do. But you must also make time for marketing, even when you're busy. And the best way to make the time is to plan for it.

The type of marketing we're focusing on in these lessons is relationship-based, referral marketing. Relationship-based marketing is all about building relationships – real relationships that fuel your business and generate clients.

(*See* Lesson 27. Marketing is about creating and nurturing real relationships. It's that simple.) Building real relationships is the most powerful thing you can do to build your business. All of the other marketing you do should support and enhance this most fundamental piece of your marketing plan. Don't get me wrong: Social media, writing, speaking – all of these things are important components of your overall marketing plan. But building relationships is the foundation for everything else.

## YOUR THREE-STEP MARKETING PLAN

**Step One: Calendar it.** To maintain an effective relationship-based marketing program, you must schedule time in your calendar. Plan at least three marketing events each week. If that sounds overwhelming, start slow and work up to three each week. Schedule one for every week this month, then two each week for next month and three each week the following month. These events can be lunches, dinners, breakfast, coffee at Starbucks, drinks after work, movies, concerts, or golf, tennis, walking, running, or bike riding. The types of event are practically endless – limited only by your imagination. I know one attorney who plans regular shopping afternoons with her best referral sources. Get creative and have fun! You're aiming for any type of event that puts you face-to-face with your best referral sources. Use these events to connect and build relationships. Enjoy yourself.

    **Step Two: Look for marketing opportunities in things you're already doing and people you already know.** I'll bet you're already doing any number of things that could be great marketing opportunities for you. Do you serve on the board of directors of a local organization? Have you taken the time to get to know the board members outside of the board meetings? Do you belong to your local Rotary Club or chamber of commerce or another club? If you do, you're surrounded by people who might be great referral sources for you. The next time you attend a board meeting, invite one of your fellow board members to breakfast or lunch. At your next bar association luncheon or Rotary Club meeting, make it a goal to meet someone new. Add them to your referral network, and follow up by inviting them out for coffee or lunch. Do whatever works for you.

As you begin this process, make sure you're including your existing network of friends, relatives and people you come in contact with on a regular basis. In *Never Eat Alone: And Other Secrets to Success, One Relationship at a Time,* [22:1] Keith Ferrazzi underscores the importance of how vast your network already is, even though you may not realize it. As you plan your marketing events think about adding the names of these people to your list:

* Relatives
* Friends of relatives
* All your spouse's relatives and contacts
* Current colleagues
* Members of professional and social organizations
* Current and former customers and clients
* Parents of your children's friends
* Neighbors, past and present
* People you went to school with
* People you have worked with in the past
* Members of your religious congregation
* Former teachers and employers
* People you socialize with
* People who provide services to you

**Step Three: Use technology.** Emails (and texts) can be great tools to help you stay connected to your network. Set aside 15 minutes, twice a week to send a few messages to your referral sources. These emails can be very short: "Hi. I was just thinking about you and wondered if we could get together. Can I give you a call to set something up? Looking forward to it." A friend, and former client of mine, will often send me a short text on holidays or a quick update about his practice or latest case outcome. I look forward to receiving his texts, and even though we don't talk often, his texts keep us connected.

Using the right technology is also essential to keeping your network organized. You can use Outlook or a case management program, or even lists that you create yourself using a service like Evernote. Find the technology that works for you, and use it!

## LIVING THE LESSON

* Schedule marketing time blocks in your calendar in three-month blocks. By doing this, you'll have already made the time for marketing, so all you need to focus on is filling up those blocks of time. If your assistant helps you plan your marketing events, then he or she can easily look in your calendar and know what times are available to schedule events for you. For example, you may block time for breakfast on Tuesdays and Thursdays and lunch on Friday. Or you might block three lunches each week. Remember, do what works for you.
* Grow your network by reaching out to people you already know professionally and personally such as board members whom you may see regularly, but don't know personally. Make sure you're including people from your current network.
* Leverage technology to create your plan and organize your contacts. There's no "best" program or service to use. The best program or service is the one that works for you.

[22:1]: Ferrazzi, Keith (2005). *Never Eat Alone: And Other Secrets to Success, One Relationship at a Time.* Crown Business.

## ADDITIONAL RESOURCES

*Evernote for Lawyers: A Guide to Getting Organized & Increasing Productivity*, by David M. Ward.

# Lesson 23

● ● ● ●

## KNOW WHERE YOUR BEST CLIENTS COME FROM AND WHY.

*Treasure your relationships, not your possessions.*

— ANTHONY J. D'ANGELO

Do you know where your best clients come from? Have you ever thought about why your best clients come to you? If you're like most attorneys, your best clients come from personal referrals. But have you ever thought about *why* your best clients come from referrals?

When someone refers a potential client to you, they are making a powerful statement about you. Your best referral sources refer people to you for three reasons:

1) They know you.
2) They like you.
3) They trust you.

Simply by giving the referral, your referral sources are telling those potential new clients that they don't just *know you*, they are telling them that they know the quality of your work and that you'll do your best for them. When someone refers a potential new client to you, they're saying that you're likeable – you're professional, friendly, and easy to work with. And most important of all, your referral source imbues you with trust. Before that potential new client ever talks to you, they trust you. They trust you because your referral source trusts you. The power of your referral sources is such that, since *they* "know, like, and trust" you, the potential clients they send your way, come to you already wanting to "know, like, and trust" you. Your job is to honor the trust your referral sources place in you.

Think about your own experience in giving referrals to other attorneys. Do you ever make referrals to attorneys you don't know, or don't like, or don't trust? The question is almost silly. No...it is silly. If you want more great clients, you've got to focus on building "know, like and trust" with your referral sources. Great referral sources are like magnets for your practice; they attract the right clients for you and send them your way. So, now you're thinking, "Okay, but how do I go about building "know, like and trust?" It's simple, and you can do it in three steps.

**Step One: get known.** Getting known is really a two-tiered process. First, get to know your referral sources. Talk with them about things other than work. Ask about their interests. Show a sincere interest in them. Do they have hobbies they love? Charities that they are passionate about? What's the best book they've read recently? Do they have kids? Dogs? Cats? Horses? I am NOT suggesting you interrogate them! I am suggesting that you look for opportunities to learn about their lives and build real relationships. Get to know them. And let them get to know you, too. Schedule time on your calendar each week to have lunch or coffee or a glass of wine with one of your best referral sources, or someone who could be a referral source for you. This investment of time is one of the best investments you can make in the profitability of your practice.

Next, you need to be known in your legal community. You need to establish yourself as a great lawyer in your practice area and build your legal chops. There are many ways to do this. The important thing is that you find a way that works for you. You can speak at legal seminars. You can host "Lunch and Learn" workshops in your office. You can write for your bar association's newsletter.

(Pro tip: Most bar association newsletter editors are hungry for submissions of thoughtful article concepts.) You can blog. You can create an e-newsletter for your firm. Find a way to get known that works for you, and just do it.

**Step Two – be likeable.** Being liked should be a natural outgrowth of getting known. As you get to know your referral sources, you'll build real relationships with them. You'll get to like them, and they'll get to like you. This won't happen with everyone you may want to cultivate as a referral source, but it WILL happen with people who will become your best referral sources.

In his book *The Likeability Factor: How to Boost Your L-Factor and Achieve Your Life's Dreams.* [23:1] Tim Sanders outlines four ways to build your "L-Factor" by enhancing four areas of your personality:

* Friendliness: Your ability to communicate openly with others.
* Relevance: Your capacity to connect with others' interests, wants, and needs.
* Empathy: Your ability to recognize and acknowledge other people's feelings.
* Realness: Your integrity which guarantees your likeability and authenticity.

*The Likeability Factor* provides some great insights and practical actions that can help you boost your "Likeability Factor," and by extension your "Referability Factor."

**Step Three – earn their trust.** The key to earning trust is acting with integrity all the time. Do what you say you are going to do. Be true to your word. Be trustworthy. When you earn the trust of your referral sources, they transfer that trust to every person they refer to you. Clients who come to you from your best referral sources already trust you because your referral source trusts you. That is powerful.

Building "know, like and trust" with people is not only important to your ability to earn more great referrals; it is essential to influencing your brand. (*See* Lesson 19. Create a great brand.)

Once you build "know, like and trust" with your referral sources, and the referrals start coming your way, there's one more thing you need to do every, single time you receive a referral: Send a thank you note to your referral source. (*See* Lesson 24. Say "thank you" for every referral.)

## LIVING THE LESSON

* Is there someone in your network you've been meaning to connect with, but you just haven't taken the time? Pick up the phone and call that person, and ask them to meet you for breakfast, or lunch, or a beer or glass of wine, or dinner. Take the first step to building the relationship. Do it. Right now.

* When you meet with your referral sources or possible referral sources, don't just talk about business. Get to know them. And let them get to know you.

* Get known in your legal community by writing or speaking. These are two of the most powerful ways you can build your reputation and credibility and "get known" as an expert in your practice area.

* Focus on friendliness. Lawyers live in an adversarial world. Sometimes it's not easy to shift out of adversarial mode. Be aware of your mood.

* Keep your commitments. To earn trust, you must be trustworthy. To be trustworthy, you must be able to keep your commitments. Start with the commitments you make to yourself. Sometimes those are the hardest to keep. If you make a promise – to yourself or anyone else – keep it.

[23:1] Sanders, Tim (2006). *The Likeability Factor: How to Boost Your L-Factor and Achieve Your Life's Dreams.* Three Rivers Press.

*Lesson 24*

●　●　●　●

# SAY "THANK YOU" FOR EVERY REFERRAL.

*Gratitude is not only the greatest of virtues,*
*but the parent of all the others.*

— *Marcus Tullius Cicero*

Remember when you were a kid and you learned to say "please" and "thank you"? If you had someone in your life who was anything like my mom, not much happened without using those "magic" words. Nowadays, I often think of the magic in the phrase "thank you." Those two, simple words, when expressed with sincere gratitude, are magical indeed. So, if you're not already in the habit of using them regularly, now's the time.

Get in the habit of saying "thank you" for every referral that comes to you. Why? When someone refers a potential client to you, they are making a powerful statement about you. Your best referral sources refer people to you for three reasons: 1) they know you; 2) they like you; and 3) they trust you. And when they refer someone to you, they're telling that person that they "know, like and trust" YOU. So, when a potential client comes to meet with you, guess what? They may not yet "know" you, and they may not yet "like" you, but one thing is certain – they come to you imbued with the trust of the person who referred them. By making the referral, your referral source is effectively saying, "I trust this attorney to do the right thing for you, and you can trust her, too." One more thing: Your referral sources are also putting their reputations on the line when they refer someone to you. They deserve a genuine thank you.

Your referral sources are treasures, and they deserve your sincere thanks for every referral they send. There are a number of things you can do to show your appreciation, but the one thing you must do is send a personal, hand-written thank you note for every referral. That being said, I understand that there are confidentiality issues to consider. You will sometimes have potential clients who don't want anyone – not even the person who referred them to your office – to know they've spoken with you, or that you've agreed to rep-resent them. That's a legitimate concern and easily addressed. At your first meeting, be sure to ask potential clients for permission to send a thank you note to your referral source, so that you don't run afoul of ethics rules in your jurisdiction. If they say they want to keep your relationship with them com-pletely confidential, don't send a thank you note. This will rarely happen, but you must respect their wishes when it does. Otherwise, send a thank you note immediately.

*Gratitude is a quality similar to electricity: it must be produced and discharged and used up in order to exist at all.*

– WILLIAM FAULKNER

## A COUPLE OF NOTES ON THANK YOU NOTES

*   You don't have to write them yourself. If your handwriting is atro-cious, ask your assistant to write the note for you. Or, if you don't like that idea, create your own template like the one on the following page – just one or two sentences – and write the note yourself. The few minutes it will take will be well worth the investment.

* Have your assistant attach a thank you note to the potential client's file at the first meeting. This will serve as a reminder to ask permission to write the note. If the answer to that question is, "yes," then you already have the note in front of you and can write it immediately at the conclusion of your first meeting.

## SAMPLE THANK YOU NOTE

Here's a sample of a simple thank you note. You can customize it for your practice. But remember: Keep it short and show genuine appreciation.

Dear Jim,

Thank you so much for referring Ms. Jones to our firm. I met with Ms. Jones this morning, and I look forward to working with her. I truly appreciate the confidence you have placed in me and my team.

Sincerely,

Barbara

## OTHER WAYS TO SHOW YOUR APPRECIATION

For your very best referral sources, you may want to do something in addition to sending a thank you note for each referral. If you really want to make an impact, make your acknowledgements personal to your referral sources. Find out what they love or what's meaningful to them, and make that part of your acknowledgment. You don't have to send a gift for every referral, just from time to time – and always with sincere and heartfelt gratitude. Here are just a few examples of personalized thank you gifts:

* A subscription to their favorite magazine
* A bottle (or case) of their favorite wine or craft beer
* A gift card to their favorite restaurant
* Tickets to a play, concert, or sporting event
* Chocolates, cookies, or other gourmet treats

* A gift card to a specialty dog or cat shop
* A donation to their favorite charity

## ONE FINAL THOUGHT

Of course you can send an email or a text or call someone to say thank you. But do these things in addition to a hand-written thank you note. Never let them be a substitute for a hand-written note.

## LIVING THE LESSON

* Use your case management system (or other software) or create a spreadsheet to track all of your potential new clients and whether thank you notes have been sent. Maintaining this database will also allow you to notice where your best clients are coming from: Who are your best referral sources? Is there a particular profession – such as CPAs or other attorneys – that sends you a lot of great clients? Be sure to capture the following information for each potential new client who contacts your office: name, date of contact with office, phone number, referral source, referral category (e.g., attorney, CPA, former client), consultation set (Y/N), thank you sent (Y/N), retained (Y/N), and matter type.
* Don't use your firm's stationery for thank you notes. Send hand-written notes. Purchase high-quality note cards such as Crane or Papyrus, or create cards customized with your firm's logo or even a personal photo. Check out www.zazzle.com or www.shutterfly.com or another service to create personalized notes. Your note doesn't have to be lengthy; two or three sentences is all you need.
* Have your assistant address the envelope and attach the envelope and card to the potential new client's file so that you have it with you during your initial meeting.
* Write the note immediately after your initial meeting.

## ADDITIONAL RESOURCES

*365 Thank Yous: The Year a Simple Act of Daily Gratitude Changed My Life,*
by John Kralik.
*The Thank You Economy,* by Gary Vaynerchuk.

## Lesson 25

•   •   •   •

# STOP TAKING "D" CLIENTS.

*I am truly impressed with your professional acumen, and
I very much want to retain you. But the other lawyer I
talked to said she could do the same work for much less.*

— IMA D. CLIENT

Lawyers are problem solvers with an innate desire to help people. Forget the lawyer jokes. The truth is that most lawyers come to the profession because they want to make a difference. Regardless of practice area, they want to help their clients. Unfortunately, this desire to help and to make a difference can blind lawyers to the dangers of the "D" client.

## WHAT'S THE DIFFERENCE BETWEEN "A" AND "D" CLIENTS?

Before we talk about identifying "D" clients, let's look at some "A" client characteristics. There are some universal characteristics that most attorneys would agree on — for example, they pay their bills, they follow your advice, they are polite to your staff, and they're not calling your office every day (or every hour). Although I speak in terms of "A" clients, you may also want to think in terms of "A" matters. For example, an "A" matter would fall within the sweet spot for your practice area; it would involve work you enjoy doing; or it might be a matter that has a high likelihood of recovery, or a high value. Have you ever thought about the characteristics of an "A" client or "A" matter for *your firm*? Some lawyers are willing to tolerate extremely difficult clients, just as long as they pay their bills or the case value is high. Other lawyers, meanwhile, simply refuse to put up with difficult clients. It's up to you.

Beyond the universal characteristics I described above, you need to understand exactly what constitutes an "A" client and an "A" matter for *you*. If you've never made these distinctions, you should. Pull out a piece of paper and write down a description of your ideal client. Be as specific as you can. Create a picture of *your* "A" client, so that you and everyone on your team knows the exact characteristics of an "A" client for your firm. If you have more than one practice area, write a description of your ideal client for each area. Do the same for ideal matters for your firm. You can't begin to attract more "A" clients without a crystal clear picture of who those "A" clients are or what those "A" matters look like.

## WHAT ARE THE WARNING SIGNS OF A "D" CLIENT?

Okay, now that you know who your ideal clients are, it's time to make room in your practice to accommodate more of them. You can start by not letting any more "D" clients into your practice and letting go of the ones you already have. And whether or not you want to admit it, you've probably got at least a few "D" clients right now. (Caveat: Be aware of your jurisdiction's ethical requirements and always let go of clients ethically, compassionately, and professionally.)

So who are these "D" clients? How do you recognize them? You already know the answers to these questions. "D" clients don't pay their bills. They are rude to your team. Maybe they're even rude to you, but they're always rude to your team. They have unrealistic expectations about their case. They don't provide the documents you request without follow-up calls and emails. They don't tell the truth. These are just a few of the characteristics of "D" clients.

Undoubtedly, you can think of many more. I'm also betting that you have a list of warning signs – bells that go off in your head – when a potential "D" client is sitting across the desk from you. Make sure the following warning signs are on your list:

* Arrives late
* Doesn't bring requested documents
* Is rude to your receptionist
* Asks first about price
* Was referred by a current "D" client
* Does not listen
* Is unrealistic about the potential outcome of the matter
* Is visibly angry or agitated
* Is currently represented and wants to make a change

Every lawyer has a "D" client from time to time. Just knowing the warning signs of "D" clients isn't enough to keep them out of your practice. Why? There are any number of answers. As discussed above, lawyers have an innate desire to help people. So, despite the warning signs, you may say "yes" to "D" clients because you KNOW you can help them. Or perhaps business has been a bit slow, so you say "yes," to a "D" client because of cash flow pressures. Whatever the reason, you need to say "no" to "D" clients because they will wreak havoc on your practice, your bottom line, and your sanity. And even worse, "D" clients steal from you. Here's what I mean.

## THE "D" CLIENT AS THIEF

"D" clients steal from you in two very damaging ways. First, they steal from you by not paying their bills. This theft is insidious because it's not just about the money – it's about the resources wasted trying to collect the money. The phone calls, the emails, the texts. The *aggravation*. The tremendous amount of effort that goes into simply getting paid for the work you've done. Clients who don't pay their bill create incredible stress in the practice and place incredible stress on you. Besides, if you're not going to get paid, wouldn't you rather not get paid for sitting on the beach or golfing or reading a good book rather than working on your "D" client's case? You should be able to choose the pro bono cases you want to take on – not have them chosen for you.

In addition to stealing your money and resources, "D" clients steal your time. Here's how. Are you familiar with the 80/20 Rule? The 80/20 Rule essentially says that 80 percent of our results come from 20 percent of our efforts. In your practice, the rule can be expressed this way: 80 percent of your revenues come from 20 percent of your clients. And guess who makes up that 20 percent? Right! Your "A" clients. Don't take my word for it; check your files. The numbers may vary slightly; 75/25 or 70/30. But you'll find that the majority of your revenues come from your "A" clients.

Here's another way the 80/20 Rule applies to your practice. Those "D" clients – the 80 percent that generate only 20 percent of your revenue – take up 80 percent of your time and your team's time. They're constantly calling, and your team has to follow up with them about everything from providing documents to paying their bills. On the other hand, those "A" clients – the ones who generate 80 percent of your revenue – respect your time. They provide documents when asked, they don't continually call or email or text, and they pay their bills. So what's wrong with this scenario? Your "D" clients are stealing from you. They're stealing the time you could be spending on more "A" clients!

Here's a simple equation to illustrate this point. Let's assume you have 100 clients who are generating $1 million in revenue. If we apply the 80/20 Rule, the analysis would look like this:

| | |
|---|---|
| 100 clients | = $1 million |
| 20 "A" Clients | = $800,000 |
| 80 others | = $200,000 |

If you were to increase the number of "A" clients in this equation by 25 percent – just five more clients in this scenario – you could replace all the revenue generated by the 80 others! While the numbers might shift a little, you get the point: Stop taking "D" clients so that you can make room in your practice for more "A" clients.

## LIVING THE LESSON

* Write down a description of your ideal "A" client(s) and matter(s). Be as specific as you can. Share the descriptions with your team. Make sure everyone understands exactly who an "A" client is for your firm.
* Do the same for "D" clients. Create a list of warning signs for "D" clients. Use the list to create a checklist that you can use as part of your client intake system.
* Pay attention. Sometimes clients can begin to slip from "A" client status during the course of representation. Regardless of the type of case or a client's level of sophistication, they are likely going through a stressful time. If a client begins to slip by being late paying the bill or being unresponsive to your office, address the matter immediately.
* Analyze the clients you already have. Make a spreadsheet or pull data from your case management program to see whether those clients on whom you're spending the most time are the clients who are generating the most revenue. You might be surprised by what you find!

*Lesson 26*

• • • •

## FEEL THE FEAR AND DO IT ANYWAY.

*You gain strength, courage, and confidence by every*
*experience in which you really stop to look fear in the face.*
*You must do the thing which you think you cannot do.*

— ELEANOR ROOSEVELT

The road to success in life is paved with change. Change – even good change – change that moves you toward your goals – can be scary. So, achieving the success you desire in life can present all sorts of scary challenges. But if you think that successful people are not afraid of change, you're wrong. Fear is natural. Fear is normal. In fact, our brains are wired to view just about any type of change as something to fear. This hardwiring can pose real problems for us because change is inevitable. Change is life. If we fear change or spend our lives trying to avoid it, we miss out on the joy of living. So, although change is inevitable, fear of change doesn't have to be. The challenge is to feel the fear and do it anyway.

People don't understand that fear is a thing. It's just another object in the universe that you are capable of experiencing. You can do one of

two things with fear: you can recognize that you have it and work to release it, or you can keep it and try to hide from it.
- From *The Untethered Soul: The Journey Beyond Yourself* [26:1]

The title of this lesson is actually the title of a book by psychologist Susan Jeffers, Ph.D., *Feel the Fear and Do It Anyway*. [26:2] These are truly words to live by. I highly recommend the book and have recommended it to many of my clients. Jeffers breaks fear down into three levels. The first level is made up of things that we fear will happen to us or require us to take action. Fears at this level include things that "happen" to us, such as aging, becoming disabled, getting fired, and losing a loved one. Other first level fears are fears that "require action" on our part, such as making decisions, changing careers, going to the doctor, and starting (or ending) a relationship. Second level fears have to do with our inner state of mind, as opposed to level one fears, which are created by external circumstances. Second level fears include rejection, success, failure, disapproval and vulnerability. Second level fears can affect every aspect of your life. For example, if you fear failure, that fear will color virtually every decision you make both personally and professionally. The level three fear is very simple. It is simply the feeling that "I can't handle it." And, according to Jeffers, it is at the root of the other two levels of fear. Level three fears transform both level one fears and level two fears.

Level one fears become:
I can't handle aging.
I can't handle becoming disabled.
I can't handle getting fired.
I can't handle losing a loved one.

Level two fears become:
I can't handle rejection.
I can't handle success.
I can't handle failure.
I can't handle disapproval.
I can't handle being vulnerable.

I read Jeffers' book for the first time more than 15 years ago, after my mom and my aunt died in an automobile accident. I was stunned by the truth of her words. Her book helped me get through the pain – and fear – that followed. That accident was an ampersand in my life. (*See* Lesson 1. This is your life. Are you living it or is it living you?) It demonstrated with intense clarity that when we leave the house in the morning, there is no guarantee we are coming back. *Feel the Fear and Do It Anyway*, helped me understand – that whatever happened – I could handle it.

I often tell my clients that my job is to help them get comfortable being uncomfortable. You've got to be able to do whatever it takes to move past your fears..."and do the thing which you think you cannot do." But how? By taking small steps to acknowledge your fear and – whatever it is – do it anyway. Jeffers offers Five Truths about fear in her book.

Truth 1. The fear will never go away as long as I continue to grow.
Truth 2. The only way to get rid of the fear of doing something is to go out and do it.
Truth 3. The only way to feel better about myself is to go out . . . and do it.
Truth 4. Not only am I going to experience fear whenever I'm on unfamiliar territory, but so is everyone else.
Truth 5. Pushing through fear is less frightening than living with the underlying fear that comes from a feeling of helplessness.

The next time you feel fear creeping up, refer to Jeffers' Five Truths About Fear, and remind yourself that you can do it. In fact, you must do it. If you don't feel the fear and do it anyway, you're likely to get caught up in a downward spiral of negative emotions. We've all been there. One thing goes wrong or we receive a piece of bad news, and suddenly, EVERYTHING feels dark.

Perhaps the biggest advance in twentieth-century psychological science was to unlock the ways in which predictable patterns of negative thinking breed negative emotions, so much so that they can even spiral down into pathological states like clinical depression, phobias, and obsessive-compulsive disorders. Negative emotions – like fear and anger – can also spawn negative thinking. This reciprocal dynamic is in fact why downward spirals are so slippery. Negative thoughts and negative emotions feed on each other. And as they do, they pull you down their abyss.

> - From *Positivity: Groundbreaking Research Reveals How to Embrace the Hidden Strength of Positive Emotions, Overcome Negativity, and Thrive*[26:3]

You have the power to change that pattern of thinking and feeling. You just need to feel the fear and do it anyway.

> *Our greatest fear should not be of failure but of succeeding at things in life that don't really matter.*
>
> — FRANCIS CHAN

## LIVING THE LESSON

* Step 1: The next time that you experience fear around something that you want to do or a change you'd like to make, feel the fear and do it anyway.
* Step 2: Congratulate yourself for taking action.
* Step 3: Repeat Step #1.

[26:1] Singer, Michael A. (2007). *The Untethered Soul: The Journey Beyond Yourself.* New Harbinger Publications / Noetic Books.
[26:2] Jeffers, Susan (1987). *Feel the Fear and Do It Anyway.* Ballantine Books.
[26:3] Fredrickson, Barbara (2008). *Positivity: Groundbreaking Research Reveals How to Embrace the Hidden Strength of Positive Emotions, Overcome Negativity, and Thrive.* Crown Archetype.

## Lesson 27

• • • •

# MARKETING IS ABOUT CREATING AND NURTURING REAL RELATIONSHIPS. IT'S THAT SIMPLE.

*Don't build links. Build relationships.*

— *RAND FISHKIN*

**A**ttorneys tell me all the time, "Nora, I'm no good at marketing. I'm just not a natural marketer. I don't like talking about myself." I tell them, "Phooey! You may not be a natural marketer, but you can learn to be an effective marketer." Before we go any further, let's define the term marketing. According to the American Marketing Association, "Marketing is the activity, set of institutions, and processes for creating, communicating, delivering, and exchanging offerings that have value for customers, clients, partners, and society at large." Whew. That is a mouthful. Here's a simpler way to say it: Marketing is about knowing what you do, knowing who your ideal clients are, and building relationships that get those clients knocking on your door.

Do you know what you do? I bet you're thinking, "Of course, I know what I do. I'm a lawyer – and a fine one, at that." Okay, but being a lawyer is part of who you are, not what you "do." As a lawyer, you guide people through some of the most difficult and challenging times of their lives. Maybe you help them survive the breakup of a marriage or a business. Maybe you help them find a way to survive after an injury leaves them unable to work or they've been illegally fired from a job. Or, perhaps you work with your clients during some of the most exciting and rewarding times of their lives. You help them create a business or launch a product. Knowing what you "do," and how you help people is critical to marketing your services. It might be difficult for you to talk about yourself, but you should be able to speak with passion about what you do for your clients. (*See* Lesson 31. Perfect your pitch. Be authentic, engaging, and powerful.)

Do you know who your ideal clients are? When you know who your ideal clients are, then you can begin to develop relationships with those people who surround your ideal clients. Let's say you're a family law attorney, and your ideal clients are successful professionals. Who are those types of people surrounded by? How about starting with financial planners, investment bankers, and business law attorneys? If you're a business lawyer, maybe your best clients are businesses such as banks or hospitals or other types of institutional clients. Think about the types of people and businesses that those institutional clients interact with on a regular basis.

Once you know who your ideal clients are and the types of people they are surrounded by, then you can get to work building relationships with the right people. You need to build real relationships that create great referrals for you. The focus here is on "real relationships," not relationships just for the purpose of getting referrals, but relationships out of which great referrals grow. In the example above, I mentioned business law attorneys as great referral sources for a family law attorney. There are plenty of business law attorneys out there. But you're not going to build relationships with all of them. You're going to meet as many business law attorneys as you can, and then, you're going to build relationships with the one, or two, or three who you really like. You're going to build real relationships with people you like, and you're going to get to know them and trust them. And they're going to get to know, like and trust you. (*See* Lesson 23. Know where your best clients come from and why.) You're going to become a great referral source for them, and they for you. It's a beautiful thing!

As you begin to build your referral relationships, think in terms of reciprocity. Reciprocity is the theory that one good turn deserves another. In *Yes!* *50 Scientifically Proven Ways to Be Persuasive*,[27:1] Robert Cialdini defines the law of reciprocity as "the social glue that helps bring people together in cooperative relationships." Always be looking for ways to help the people in your referral network.

Another simple way to activate the law of reciprocity is to ask for favors. By asking for favors, you're giving people the opportunity to help you. Having the ability to genuinely help someone makes us feel good. So look for opportunities to ask for favors in a genuine way. Be sincere and straightforward. And you don't have to ask someone to actually do something for you, although you can. You can ask for help, advice or suggestions. In D.A. Benton's book, *Executive Charisma*,[27:2] Benton notes that when you ask for favors, you give people the opportunity to be useful and *feel* useful. When you ask, keep it simple, be specific, and always say thank you. Benton suggests the following approach: "Would you do me a favor...I'd be grateful, if you would..." and later, "Thank you." And when you're asked to do a favor for someone, be responsive. If you can help them out, do it.

*If you want to make a friend, let someone do you a favor.*

— BEN FRANKLIN

## LIVING THE LESSON

* Get clear about what you do and how you help your clients. Then start drafting your Elevator Pitch. Write it down. (*See* Lesson 31. Perfect your pitch. Be authentic, engaging, and powerful.)
* Know who your ideal clients are so that you can begin to create and nurture relationships with those people who surround and influence them.

*   Build relationships by activating the law of reciprocity and asking for favors. Be genuine, and always say thank you.

[27:1] Goldstein, Noah J., Martin, Steve J., and Cialdini, Robert B., Ph.D. (2009). *Yes! 50 Scientifically Proven Ways to Be Persuasive.* Free Press.
[27:2] Benton, D.A. (2005). *Executive Charisma: Six Steps to Mastering the Art of Leadership.* McGraw-Hill.

*Lesson 28*

● ● ● ●

# BE THE HOST, NOT THE GUEST.

*There is no cure for birth and death save to enjoy the interval.*

— GEORGE SANTAYANA

Parties, receptions, seminars, workshops and other types of networking [READ: relationship building] opportunities are often not really networking opportunities at all. Why? Because most of the time we gravitate toward people we already know, and, in doing so, we miss the chance to meet new people.

Why? First and foremost is that we're all more comfortable around people we know. Or maybe you're more introverted than extroverted, so it's not easy for you to step out of your comfort zone at events. Whatever the reason, you've got to find a way through it. Why? Because you're going to go to a considerable number of parties and receptions and seminars and workshops during your career. So, why not make the most out of these opportunities to market your practice?

I'm not saying that when you go to an event you should ignore the folks you already know. Of course, not. But reconnecting with friends at events is the easy part for most of us. I'm saying that to get the most out of attending an event, you might have to step out of your comfort zone.

*We're fools whether we dance or not, so we might as well dance.*

— JAPANESE PROVERB

## FIVE WAYS TO GET THE MOST OUT OF ATTENDING ANY EVENT

### 1. Make it a game.

Think of every event you attend as a game in which you get to set the rules. Set a goal for the number of new relationships you'd like to create. Notice I didn't say the number of people you'd like to meet. You may meet a dozen people at an event. That doesn't mean you're going to actually get to know all of those people. Set a goal for creating new relationships with just a few people at each event. Just one real relationship is more valuable than 10 business card exchanges. You should also set a goal for the number of introductions you'd like to make. If you know two people who you think would benefit from knowing each other, introduce them. Connecting people by making introductions is a wonderful way to not only be of service, but to also build your network.

### 2. Be the host, not the guest.

The next time you go to a marketing event, don't think of yourself as a guest. Instead, think of yourself as the host. When you think of yourself as the host, your focus and perspective shift. By simply "being the host," you change your entire persona. I read this sage piece of advice in *Don't Keep Me a Secret: Proven Tactics to Get More Referrals and Introductions,* [28:1] by Bill Cates. "Being the host" forces you to step out more. Yes, perhaps even a bit beyond your comfort zone. So get out there and "be the host." Here are some specific examples from *Don't Keep Me a Secret* that illustrate the difference.

| Guest | Host |
|---|---|
| Takes a passive role | Takes an active role |
| More reserved | More outgoing |
| Waits to be introduced | Takes initiative |
| Often feels awkward | Helps others feel relaxed |
| Waits to be approached | Initiates conversations |
| Waits for an invitation to activities | Helps facilitate activities |
| Stays in one place | Mingles, makes introductions |

## 3. Be ready with a few good questions.

There are a few initial questions that typically start a conversation: "What do you do?" Or, if you're with a group of other lawyers, "What's your practice area?" "Where are you from?" "What firm are you with?" These questions may get a conversation started, but where do you go from there? Questions are a wonderful way to really get to know someone. You should have a few favorites to ask the new folks you meet. Here are some of my favorites:

**For other lawyers:**

* Why did you go to law school?
* Why did you choose your practice area?
* Who is your ideal client? This is a great question because it allows you to begin building a referral relationship, and it can be asked of any professional – not just lawyers.

**For non-lawyers:**

* What do you think is the coming trend in your industry/profession?
* What do you enjoy most about your work?

\*   What advice would you give someone just starting out in your industry/profession?

A note about asking questions: Asking questions at a networking event should not be approached as a cross-examination. Ask questions with sincerity and with a genuine desire to learn more about the person. If you're asking questions just to manipulate the conversation, the other person will know it, and will likely make a mad dash for the exit.

## 4. Listen.

Once you've asked the right questions, listen. (*See* Lesson 35. Learn how to listen. Really listen.) This is a tough one. Lawyers are taught to listen in order to prepare their response. The only time that type of lawyerly listening is appropriate is when you are acting as an advocate for your client. Instead, listen with a focus on really hearing what the other person is saying. DO NOT scan the room for other people you may want to connect with. Give the person you're talking with your full attention. If you do, you will make a tremendously positive impact on them and on the relationship.

> People will tolerate all sorts of rudeness, but the inability to pay attention holds a special place in their hearts—perhaps because it's something all of us should be able to do with ease. After all, what's it take to keep our ears open, our eyes looking at whoever's talking, and our mouths shut?
> - From *What Got You Here, Won't Get You There: How Successful People Become Even More Successful*[28:2]

## 5. Follow up

Remember that when you leave the event, it is not over. You've got to follow up with the people you've met. Your goal should be to meet just a few people with whom you want to create relationships. So, follow-up should come naturally. If you don't follow up, everything else you've done up to this point has been a waste of your time.

## LIVING THE LESSON

* Set a goal for the next event you attend. Do you want to create relationships with two new people? Do you want to create a relationship with someone in a particular profession? An attorney in a different practice area?
* Practice "being the host," at every networking event you attend. Don't sit with people you already know. Find a spot next to someone you've never met and introduce yourself.
* Create your own favorite questions.
* Listen. Really listen.
* Follow up as soon as possible. Make it a habit to follow up with the people you meet the very next day. If you wait for more than a day, you will likely forget to follow up at all. How you follow up is your decision and will depend upon the conversation you had. You may want to call the person to set up a lunch. Or, perhaps send them an email attaching an article or blog post that would be of interest to them. Or, maybe you'll want to send them an invitation to connect on LinkedIn. How you follow up is up to you. Just be sure you do it!

[28:1] Cates, Bill (2007). *Don't Keep Me a Secret: Proven Tactics to Get Referrals and Introductions.* McGraw-Hill.
[28:2] Goldsmith, Marshall (2007). *What Got You Here, Won't Get You There: How Successful People Become Even More Successful.* Hyperion.

## ADDITIONAL RESOURCES

*76 Ways to Build a Straight Referral Business A.S.A.P.*, by Lorna Riley.

## Lesson 29

● ● ● ●

# JOIN THE SOCIAL MEDIA CONVERSATION. TEACH – DON'T SELL.

*Social media is no longer an option for your small and medium sized law firms, it's critical for your success.*

– KEVIN O'KEEFE, FOUNDER OF LEXBLOG

*If you don't like change, you're going to like irrelevance even less.*

—GENERAL ERIC SHINSEKI, RETIRED
CHIEF OF STAFF, U. S. ARMY

Lawyers are not the earliest of adopters when it comes to, well, just about anything. Social media is no exception. But the reality is that social media is here to stay. So you can either embrace the change or not. It's your choice.

Social media has fundamentally changed the way we connect and communicate. So if you want to thrive in the years to come or, at the very least, not become irrelevant, you've got to embrace it.

Although many lawyers were late to the social media party, their numbers are growing. In fact, the number of lawyers using social media has risen dramatically in the past four years. According to the American Bar Association's 2014 Legal Technology Survey Report, 62% of respondents reported that they use networks such as Facebook, Twitter, or LinkedIn, compared to 55% in 2012, 43% in 2011, and 17% in 2010. According to a study by LinkedIn reported in February 2014, 81% of small and medium businesses surveyed use social media.

> *75% of B2B decision makers use social media*
> *to learn. Be a teacher – not a seller.*
>
> *— Gerry Moran, Head of Social Media*
> *at SAP North America*

## CHANGE HOW YOU THINK ABOUT SOCIAL MEDIA.

Don't think of social media networks as merely marketing tools for your firm. Instead, think of them as learning tools for your clients, potential clients and referral sources. Social networks have created new ways of communicating with your referral sources, current clients, and even potential clients. On a broad scale, social media allows you to establish your credibility, share your knowledge, and be viewed as a trusted advisor. Social networks give you the opportunity to expand your influence far beyond your local community. And although social media is not a replacement for relationship marketing, it will support and enhance the personal marketing you do. Social media allows you to build your brand in a variety of ways.

**Expand your network.** Social media gives you the ability to create relationships with people you would never be able to connect with otherwise. You can connect with people all over the world. You never know where that next "A" client might come from. I've worked with more than one attorney who has generated "A" clients as a result of a robust presence on LinkedIn.

**Build your credibility.** Use social media to educate your followers. Give useful knowledge away through articles, blog posts, and white papers. Post articles you've written or articles that would be of interest to your network. The greater your presence on the Web, the more credibility you have. Social media lets you become THE source for news in your practice area. LinkedIn and other social networks make it easy to share articles from a wide variety of news sources.

**Start relationships online; follow-up offline.** When you connect with people on LinkedIn or follow people on Twitter or comment on interesting blog posts, you're opening the door to not just online communication, but offline, real-world relationships. If you connect with someone in your city, ask them if they'd like to get together for coffee so that you can learn more about their business. If your connection is in another part of the state or country, look for opportunities to connect with them when you're traveling.

## FINDING THE TIME TO GET SOCIAL.

Let's face it, as powerful as social media is, it can also be a huge time waster. It's easy to feel overwhelmed by a flood of information. So make sure you do all that you can to avoid social media burnout:

* Create a social media plan. What are your objectives? What networks do you want to participate in? LinkedIn is a must for lawyers. But you should also consider Facebook, Twitter, and Google+. Do you want to start a blog? Blogging can be incredibly valuable, but it also requires a significant time commitment.
* Budget and block your time depending upon your objectives. Plan on a couple of hours a week to get started.
* Get help. For example, if you blog, enlist the help of young associates, virtual assistants, or law school interns to research topics for you. They can even write drafts for you. But unless you find a fantastic writer who understands your voice, write the final product yourself.
* Use online tutorials. LinkedIn has an excellent help center.
* Use social media tools like www.HootSuite.com or www.Buffer.com. These tools let you organize all of your social media accounts in one place and schedule updates and tweets in advance.

* Post content on the weekend. According to www.MarketingProfs.com, content posted on the weekend is shared more often than content posted during the week.

* Give yourself a couple of social media breaks each day. Spend a few minutes in the morning and a few minutes in the afternoon checking in on your networks. Share an update on LinkedIn or comment on a discussion in one of the groups you belong to. Post an update to your firm's Facebook page. You can share a post from someone you follow or link to an article that would be of interest to your followers.

* Mix up your posts. Make sure that you're not just sharing information. Be sure to comment on posts by other people and reply to comments on things you've posted. And from time to time, share something personal. If you love dogs, share something about dogs. If you love wine, share a link about one of your favorites. People want to get to know you. Let them.

* Here are rules of thumb for posting, from *Social Media for Lawyers: The Next Frontier:*[29:1]

    o 40%: Links to articles and blogs of interest to your network. Retweets and shares from your network. Remember, your goal is to teach, not sell. Sharing valuable articles and information from others is a great way to establish yourself as a trusted advisor.

    o 30%: Replies and comments to other people's posts or your own.

    o 20%: Self-promotion like your upcoming webinar or other accomplishments.

    o 10% Personal Stuff – dogs, wine, fitness, sailing, food. Stuff you love outside the practice of law.

## GETTING STARTED

The suggestions below are focused on LinkedIn, but the concepts apply to any social network: Listen. Find your niche. Connect and teach. Build your network.

**Listen.** Before you join the conversation, spend some time listening. Learn what's important to the people in your network. Do you do a lot of construction litigation? Join one of the construction law groups or other construction-focused groups on LinkedIn. Notice what topics are of interest to the members of the group.

**Find your niche.** Your practice area creates a natural niche for you. Share information and articles relevant to your potential "A" clients. For many practice areas, your ideal clients are already on LinkedIn.

**Build Your Network.** Start building your network by reaching out to people you already know. Connect with members of your groups who post articles or who start discussions you find interesting.

**Connect and teach.** Focus on teaching and sharing information.

## A FEW WORDS ABOUT ETHICS.

The world of social media is moving much faster than bar associations' ability to regulate it. Focus on teaching and sharing information, and you'll steer clear of most ethical pitfalls. That being said, you must know your jurisdiction's advertising rules, and never use social media to solicit clients.

> Use of social media doesn't transform otherwise appropriate conduct into something unethical.
> - From *Social Media for Lawyers: The Next Frontier*

## LIVING THE LESSON

* Create your social media plan. Decide what networks to join and how much time you'll spend each week on social media.
* Build social media breaks into your day. Schedule time in your calendar to check in on your networks.
* Set goals and measure your progress.
* Have fun.

[29:1] Black, Nicole and Elefant, Carolyn (2010). *Social Media for Lawyers: The Next Frontier.* American Bar Association.

## ADDITIONAL RESOURCES

*Trust Agents: Using the Web to Build Influence, Improve Reputation and Earn Trust,* by Chris Brogan and Julien Smith.

*The Art of Social Media: Power Tips for Power Users,* by Guy Kawasaki and Peg Fitzpatrick.

*The Social Media Management Handbook: Everything You Need to Know to get Social Media Working in Your Business,* by Nick Smith, Robert Wollan, Catherine Zou.

*Lesson 30*

●  ●  ●  ●

# GET SOME SLEEP.

*But I have promises to keep, and miles to go*
*before I sleep, and miles to go before I sleep.*

— *Robert Frost*

That quote is from one of my favorite poems, "Stopping by the Woods on a Snowy Evening." I've always loved the beautiful images Frost drew with his words. Now, when I see that quote, I can't help but think about how relevant it seems to life today. So often, we feel that there are miles to go before we sleep. There is always one more thing to do. And as a result, we are a sleep-deprived culture.

In a 2013 study conducted by Gallup, researchers found that 40 percent of Americans get fewer than seven hours of sleep each night. And 43 percent reported that they would feel better with more sleep.[30:1] Perhaps unsurprisingly, Gallup's research showed that the number of hours we sleep has decreased in recent decades. Gallup didn't single out lawyers in its research, but I'd bet that law is among the most sleep-deprived professions in the country. Lawyers live in a culture that for decades has said, "Work long, work late, no matter what you're working on."

Although the amount of sleep someone needs to be at their best varies, the National Sleep Foundation recommends an average of seven to nine hours per night for adults over age 18. Science cannot prescribe the exact amount of sleep a person needs. But what science can tell us, according to researcher and molecular biologist John Medina, is that not getting enough sleep is really bad for us. Medina is the author of *Brain Rules: 12 Principles for Surviving and Thriving at Work, Home and School*.[30:2] Medina's Brain Rule #7 is all about sleep, and the title of that chapter says it all: Sleep well, think well.

*The best bridge between despair and hope is a good night's sleep.*

— E. JOSEPH LOSSMAN

But before we talk about why a lack of sleep is bad for us, let's take a quick look at all the good things sleep does for us. There are tremendous amounts of research that demonstrate the value of a good night's sleep. Sleep boosts our capacity for learning. It supports the executive function of our brain which is critical to decision-making. Sleep helps us process and organize our memories and experiences so that we can call upon them later. And sleep doesn't have to occur just during the night. Naps boost our brain power, too. One NASA sleep study reported by Medina in *Brain Rules* showed that "a 26-minute nap improved a pilot's performance by more than 34 percent."

*No day is so bad it can't be fixed with a nap.*

— CARRIE SNOW

Getting enough sleep produces tons of cognitive benefits, not to mention, you just feel better when you've had enough sleep. Unfortunately, lack of sleep – especially chronic sleep debt which is the cumulative effect of not getting enough sleep –can be disastrous for our brains. In *Brain Rules*, Medina catalogs a litany of problems caused by not getting enough sleep. One study found that certain body chemistries of healthy 30-year-olds allowed to sleep only about four hours a night for six consecutive nights looked more like the body chemistries of 60-year-olds. And, when they were allowed to return to their normal sleep patterns, it took them almost a week to return to their 30-year-old systems!

The bottom line is that sleep loss means mind loss. Sleep loss cripples thinking, in just about every way you can measure thinking. Sleep loss hurts attention, executive function, immediate memory, working memory, mood, quantitative skills, logical reasoning ability, general math knowledge. Eventually, sleep loss affects manual dexterity, including fine motor control ... and even gross motor movements, such as the ability to walk on a treadmill.
  - From *Brain Rules: 12 Principles for Surviving and Thriving at Work, Home, and School*

So, if you want to be a better lawyer, get some sleep.

*Finish each day before you begin the next, and interpose a solid wall of sleep between the two.*

– Ralph Waldo Emerson

## LIVING THE LESSON

* If you're not sure how much sleep is the right amount for you, keep a journal and note how much sleep you've had when you feel your best.
* Create good sleep habits.
  o Turn off electronics – phones, tablets, and computers – at least 30 minutes before going to sleep.
  o Keep your bedroom dark. Even the light from electronic clocks can disturb your sleep.
  o Keep your bedroom cool. Sleep research says that we sleep better when we're just slightly cool.

\*    Visit the National Sleep Foundation (www.sleepfoundation.org) for more information on how to get a good night's sleep.

[30:1] Jones, Jeffrey M. (2013). *In U.S., 40% Get Less Than Recommended Amount of Sleep.* Gallup. Retrieved from: http://www.gallup.com/poll/166553/less-recommended-amount-sleep.aspx

[30:2] Medina, John (2010). *Brain Rules: 12 Principles for Surviving and Thriving at Work, Home and School.* Pear Press.

## ADDITIONAL RESOURCES

Check out John Medina's website: www.brainrules.net.

## Lesson 31

● ● ● ●

# PERFECT YOUR PITCH. BE AUTHENTIC, ENGAGING, AND POWERFUL.

*People don't buy what you do, they buy why you do it.*

— SIMON SINEK

What do you do? Your answer to that question can make all the difference in the world to your practice. Your answer can leave people saying politely, "Nice to meet you." Or your answer can be met with an enthusiastic, "Wow. Tell me more about your firm," or "I'd love to learn more; let's have coffee soon."

Let me ask you another question: Why do you do what you do? I know that may sound like a crazy question. But when was the last time you thought about why you do what you do? Why did you choose to become an attorney? Why do you practice in the area of law that you do? Why do you come to the office every day? When you think about creating your elevator pitch, WHY is the perfect place to start. Here's why.

Most attorneys can speak about WHAT they do. They litigate. They help people create estate plans. They work on real estate deals. They draft contracts. It makes perfect sense to know what you do and to be able to speak about it. When you meet someone at a party, they ask, "So, WHAT do you do?" They don't ask, "So, tell me WHY do you do what you do?" But, if they did ask that question, how would you answer?

Most attorneys can also speak about HOW they do what they do. They can speak to you about their team. They may even speak in terms of value and what makes their firm unique. These things are important. And don't get me wrong, you should be able to speak authentically about WHAT you do and HOW you do it. But before you get to the WHAT and the HOW, you should know WHY you do what you do AND be able to tell people – right up front.

According to David Yewman, co-author of *Weekend Language*[31:1] and co-founder of ElevatorSpeech, a consulting firm that specializes in helping clients craft 30-second descriptions of their companies, "Executives who can't, in a half a minute, explain what they do and why anyone should care, miss out – on sales, funding, partnerships and more opportunities."

Attorneys who can't explain why they do what they do and how they help their clients in 30 seconds without using jargon or legalese miss out on referrals. It's that simple. "You've got to cut right to it, hit them over the head with it. The magic comes when you can talk like a human being about your business, and when you can really deliver a punch on why this is important," says Yewman.

Why is WHY so important? Because so few people – or businesses – can explain why they do what they do, and those who can have a distinct advantage over those who can't. In his book, *Start with Why: How Great Leaders Inspire Everyone to Take Action,*[31:2] author Simon Sinek makes a powerful case for the power of WHY.

Sinek studied how great leaders communicate and created the concept of "The Golden Circle." Think in terms of three concentric circles. The outermost circle is the "what." Any person or company can tell you WHAT they do. The middle circle is the "how." The HOW is a bit trickier, and most companies explain HOW they do what they do by differentiating themselves from the competition. At the core of The Golden Circle is the WHY. Your WHY is your purpose. Your WHY is what you believe. The WHY for any business is not to make money. Money is the result of why you do what you do. Money and profits flow from WHY you do what you do.

## START WITH WHY

In his book, *Start with Why*, Sinek's core message is: "People don't buy what you do, they buy why you do it."

> Very few people or companies can clearly articulate WHY they do WHAT they do. When I say WHY, I don't mean to make money— that's a result. By WHY I mean what is your purpose, cause or belief? WHY does your company exist? WHY do you get out of bed every morning? And WHY should anyone care? . . . But when a company clearly communicates their WHY, what they believe, and we believe what they believe, then we will sometimes go to extraordinary lengths to include those products or brands in our lives.
> – From *Start with Why*

## WHY PEOPLE HATE MOST ELEVATOR SPEECHES.

You need to be able to explain your business to anyone who asks in a way that is authentic, engaging and powerful. Why? Because if you can't speak about why you do what you do in a way that is authentic, engaging and powerful, who can? And what's more, if you can't speak about why you do what you do in a way that's authentic, engaging and powerful, why would anyone want to work with you?

But the typical lawyer's elevator speech is rarely authentic, engaging, and powerful. (YOU are not the typical lawyer.) All too often, what we refer to as elevator speeches are more like monologues that either drone on for what seems like an eternity or are filled with cutesy clichés and professional jargon – or both. To wit:

"Hi. What do you do?"

"I'm a commercial litigator. I've been in practice for 25 years, and my firm works with all types of businesses when they are sued in circuit or federal court. We handle complex litigation matters including fraud in business transactions, breach of contract, non-competition and non-solicitation agreements, tortious interference with contracts and breaches of fiduciary duty. We also counsel our clients in every aspect of business creation and incorporation. Yada…yada…yada… blah…blah…blah…"

[Yawn] "Nice meeting you."

That is not the response you want. Part of the problem is the question itself: "What do you do?" When we answer the question "What do you do?" we focus on the nuts and bolts – the facts. Lawyers love to focus on facts, but facts are not what should drive your elevator pitch. Rather than explaining WHAT you do by discussing facts, talk about WHY you do what you do. When you talk about why you do what you do, you'll engage your emotions and the emotions of the person you're speaking with. People are driven by emotions, not facts. So if you want your elevator pitch to really resonate with people and to grab their attention, appeal to their emotions – with emotion.

In *Brain Rules: 12 Principles for Surviving and Thriving at Work, Home and School*,[31:3] author and molecular biologist John Media points to scientific studies that demonstrate time after time that emotions get our attention – not facts. So if you launch into an elevator pitch all about "what you do" devoid of emotion and passion, your message will not get through, and you're much more likely to hear, "Nice meeting you," than, "Let's get together for coffee. I want to learn more about your firm." Starting with why helps you infuse your pitch with real emotion.

Here's another typical response to the question, "What do you do?" from a family law attorney:

"I've been practicing in the area of Family Law for over 20 years. My staff is also very experienced, and we focus on handling our cases as efficiently and effectively as possible. We're proud to provide excellent client service."

Now here's an elevator pitch for the same family law attorney, but this pitch starts with WHY.

"You know why I love being a family law attorney? Every day everyone in my office comes to work knowing that we are going to make a difference in the lives of the people we work with. Getting divorced is really rough and every single one of us is committed to helping our clients and their families move through the process with as little pain as possible."

If you were making a referral to a Family Law attorney, who would you choose? How would your elevator pitch sound if you started with WHY? I bet it would be better.

## CARDINAL RULES FOR YOUR PITCH

* Talk like a person.
* NO legalese or jargon.
* Keep it simple.

## LIVING THE LESSON

* **Answer the question: Why do you do what you do?**
  Brainstorm the answer to that question for yourself. Another way to think of the question is: What is my purpose? What do I stand for? What does our firm stand for?
* **Write it out.**
  Write out your answer to the question. Think about it. Carry what you've written down around with you and reflect on it. Do the words ring true for you? Do they make you feel excited about the work you do? If not, keep working. Don't stop until you've created an elevator pitch that you are proud to shout from the rooftops.
* **Practice, practice, practice.**
  Once you've written your elevator pitch, practice it. One of the best ways to practice it is to record yourself speaking it. Use your phone to record yourself, then listen back. Do you sound authentic? Do you sound engaging and passionate? Do you sound like you believe in

what you do? If not, keep working on it. YOU are a lawyer. YOU transform people's lives. YOU make a difference. If you can't speak with power and passion about why you do what you do, who will?

*   **Test it.**

    Once you're comfortable with your pitch, test it on people you know. Get very comfortable speaking it. Ask for feedback. Make adjustments, and practice, practice, practice.

*   **Refine it.**

    Your elevator pitch is dynamic. You should be constantly working to refine and improve it. And if you have more than one practice area, you should have more than one elevator pitch.

[31:1] Yewman, David, and Craig, Andy (2013). *Weekend Language*: Presenting with More Stories and Less PowerPoint. DASH Consulting, Incorporated.

[31:2] Sinek, Simon (2011). Start with Why: How Great Leaders Inspire Everyone to Take Action. Penguin Group.

[31:3] Medina, John (2009). *Brain Rules: 12 Principles for Surviving and Thriving at Work, Home and School.* Pear Press.


## ADDITIONAL RESOURCES

*BRAG! The Art of Tooting Your Own Horn Without Blowing It,* by Peggy Klaus.

## Lesson 32

● ● ● ●

# SEE YOUR FIRM THROUGH YOUR CLIENTS' EYES. CREATE A UNIQUE EXPERIENCE.

*While we are a coffee company at heart, Starbucks provides much more than the best cup of coffee – we offer a community gathering place where people come together to connect and discover new things.*

*– HOWARD SCHULTZ*

Starbucks doesn't just sell coffee. Starbucks sells "the Starbucks experience." Everything about their stores is designed to make their customers feel welcome and comfortable. In 1983, Starbucks CEO Howard Shultz traveled to Italy and experienced Italian coffee bars. Then and now, these cafés are not merely places to purchase coffee; rather, they are where Italians go to relax, meet friends, read, and chat with other customers and the baristas. Shultz was so taken with the cafés of Italy that he decided to model Starbucks after them. Schultz's vision for Starbucks was for it to be "the third place." Like the cafés of Italy, Starbucks would be a place to go between home and work.

Starbucks knows the value of creating an experience for its customers. It's not just about the coffee. It's about the way the stores look, the comfy chairs, the music that's playing, the smells of freshly brewed coffee, the baristas who know you by name and, if you're a regular, they know your favorite drink. By creating "the Starbucks experience," Starbucks has elevated a simple commodity like coffee, which in some places sells for less than a dollar a cup, to an experience. A Starbucks customer thinks nothing of paying four or five dollars – or more – for their special coffee drink.

So what does this have to do with your law firm? Plenty. In their book, *The Experience Economy,*[32:1] Joe Pine and James Gilmore discuss the evolution of our economy from one that is commodity-based through today's experience-based model. Or from coffee as beans, selling at a few cents to a dollar a pound through coffee as an experience: a Venti hazelnut latte with light foam, served with free Wi-Fi and comfy chairs for five dollars. Pine and Gilmore argue that if businesses in the 21$^{st}$ century are not delivering experiences to their customers, they are losing and will continue to lose. But, according to Pine and Gilmore, experiences are not the final step in economic evolution. Beyond the experience economy is the transformation economy. At this level, an experience is customized to provide exactly what the customer needs. This is the final evolutionary step in the economy, at least for the foreseeable future.

Think about that for a minute. You and your law firm, by virtue of the work you do every day, are already in the business of transforming people's lives. People come to you with a problem, and you help them. When the matter is concluded, something in the client's life or business has been changed, transformed. Yet every day, new online legal services like LegalZoom and RocketLawyer are commoditizing the practice of law. Your job is to create an experience for your clients that cannot be replicated by an online service. Start shifting how you think about your law firm and the work that you do. Start asking the questions: How can we offer a positive experience to our clients? In what ways do we transform the lives and businesses of the people we work with?

*I've learned that people will forget what you*
*said, people will forget what you did, but people*
*will never forget how you made them feel.*

*– MAYA ANGELOU*

And if you think this is all just touchy-feely mumbo jumbo, I have a story for you. I'll never forget a conversation I had at a bar association reception I attended. While I stood in line at the bar, the husband of one of the lawyers in attendance began chatting with me. He was an entrepreneur who had just lost a sizeable amount of money in a business deal. "It's been really rough," he said, "But those kinds of risks are part of the business." He didn't go into specific details, but I could see that this situation was really wearing on him. "You know what bothers me almost as much as the deal going south?" he asked. "No," I replied. "My lawyer hasn't even called me since the last meeting. He hasn't even called to see how I'm doing. He did the best he could, and I told him I don't blame him for what went wrong. But don't you think he could pick up the phone and give me a call?" Whether or not they tell you, your clients want to know you care about them.

The experience this man went through certainly transformed his life, and not in a positive way. But how might his situation have been different? How might his "experience" of his relationship with his lawyer have been different? Could his lawyer have done anything to make this "transformation" less painful? Yes. Simply showing that you care is a powerful way to enhance the experience – good or bad – that a client has with your firm.

## WHAT ARE YOU DOING TO BE BETTER THAN STARBUCKS?

When you envision yourself and your law practice, what do you see? Are you creating YOUR firm, or are you just recreating what thousands of lawyers before you have done? What do your clients experience when they interact with your law firm? Are you doing everything you can to create a positive experience? Are you constantly asking yourself these questions: How can we serve our clients better? How can we make bad experiences easier on them, and how can we elevate good experiences so that clients feel transformed? If you've never answered these questions, now is the time.

Here's an example of an office providing a positive and unique client experience in the reception area:

* The office is neat and impeccably decorated in a way that reflects your style.
* The receptionist treats everyone who enters with warmth and kindness.
* Free wireless internet is provided.
* Freshly baked Otis Spunkmeyer cookies or pastries are available.
* There is a Keurig coffee maker with Starbucks K-cups, of course.
* Music is playing in the background.
* There are digital photo frames or TV screens with information about the firm and the people who work there.

Your list might look different, but you get the idea. So get busy. Get going. Start today transforming your law firm to one that is part of the new economy – the transformation economy.

## LIVING THE LESSON

* Ask everyone on your team: "How can we serve our clients better?"
* Get input from everyone, and make a list of suggested changes.
* Categories to consider:
   o Physical office space
   o How we handle phone calls
   o How we process emails
   o How clients are greeted
   o How appointments are scheduled
   o How our bills and invoices look
   o How we price our services
   o How we close our files or matters

[32:1] Pine, Joseph P. II, and Gilmore, James H. (2011). *The Experience Economy*. Harvard Business Review Press.

## Lesson 33

● ● ● ●

# HATE MARKETING? DO WHAT YOU LOVE.

*If you are not doing what you love, you are wasting your time.*

— BILLY JOEL

We all have some things in our lives that we just hate doing. And when it comes to marketing, that usually means going to some type of event that you really don't enjoy. There is nothing quite as painful as going to a [fill in what's true for you] because you feel like you have to. But you go anyway. You skulk around. Well, you probably don't feel like you're skulking, but that's the effect you have on the other folks there. You're miserable. You don't act like the host of the event. (*See* Lesson 28. Be the host, not the guest.) You don't even act like a guest. You're more like a hostage. You don't meet any new people. You don't engage in any fun or meaningful conversations. You have a drink, chat with a few folks you know, and head for the door. Then when no referrals come, you think to yourself, "I knew that was going to be a waste of my time."

Well you're right. If you're doing things you hate doing just because you think you have to in order to market your firm, here's some advice: STOP IT! It's like the old joke:

Patient: Doctor, it hurts when I do this. [Lifting arm, bending knee or some other function.]
Doctor: Then stop doing that!

If what you're doing to market your practice is painful for you, stop it. Instead, do what you love. Focus on what you love doing and do more of it.

Here's what I mean. If you're a member of an organization because you think you have to be in order to market your firm, you're wrong. In fact, if you hate attending [insert organization name here] meetings, the likelihood of your meeting great referral sources there is slim. Why? Because the moment you arrive, you're thinking of how soon you can leave. You give off an aura of "I don't want to be here," and everyone around you knows it. So, making new connections and building great relationships in that kind of atmosphere is nearly impossible. And remember: The key to building your practice is building relationships.

When you do what you love, you bring your whole self to the activity. You're enthusiastic. You're engaged. You're more approachable, and people will gravitate toward you. It doesn't matter if you're shy or introverted; if you do what you love, you'll be comfortable.

Find organizations that are meaningful to you and get involved. Is there a local nonprofit organization or cause that you care deeply about? Reach out and volunteer. You could also offer to serve on their board of trustees. Most nonprofit organizations truly appreciate having lawyers on their boards.

Is there an activity or sport that you're passionate about? Think of ways you can turn that activity into a marketing opportunity. What could be better than doing what you love and turning it into an opportunity to market your firm? Here are just a few ideas:

Boating: Do you love being out on the water? Chances are some of your best referral sources love it, too. Create a monthly boating date for you and them. Boating is a wonderful way to get to know your referral sources. And invite them to bring their husband, wife, significant other – even their kids. It's up to you.

Wine: If you're a wine aficionado, you've got the perfect reason to throw a party. Invite colleagues, friends, and referral sources to a personalized wine tasting. You can host it in your home or at your office.

Beer: Craft beer breweries are popping up everywhere. Some people might even say, "Beer is the new wine." If you love beer, why not host a party at your local craft brewery?

Cooking: If you fancy yourself the next Thomas Keller or Giada De Laurentiis, host a dinner party in your home. Breaking bread is a special way to get to know the people who are most important to your practice.

Movies: If you're a movie buff, you can rent a theater for a special showing. Renting a movie theater for a private screening is more affordable than you might think. And just think of the options – from *To Kill a Mockingbird* to *My Cousin Vinnie!*

Running or bike riding: Sponsor a run or a ride for your favorite charity. Or put together a team to take part in a scheduled run or ride. You can do the same if you love motorcycle riding.

Shopping: I know one lawyer who plans regular shopping days with her best referral sources. They shop. They do lunch. They have fun together. THAT is what it's all about.

A good friend and lawyer from Kentucky hosted a Kentucky Derby party at his house in Florida for years. It was the hottest ticket in town when Derby Day rolled around. He lined his driveway with flags that matched the colors of the jockey's silks. He had bartenders making mint juleps. He put out a tremendous spread of food, including Derby pies, and he even made his own burgoo (a Kentucky stew). The first Derby parties he threw were just for friends and relatives. Then he decided to turn the party into a marketing event for his firm. The first year that he invited his colleagues and referral sources, there were over a hundred people there. He had a blast and so did everyone else.

Marketing doesn't have to be painful. No...marketing should *never* be painful. Find a way to turn what you already love doing into a way to market your firm. You'll love it.

## LIVING THE LESSON

* Make a list of your hobbies, sports you love, causes that you feel passionate about. Write everything down, even if you think you could never use your passion as a marketing activity.
* Brainstorm with your family and your team at the office to decide on an activity or event that you'd like to use for marketing the firm.
* Let your team at the office help you plan, organize, and pull off your marketing event. I guarantee you that they'll have fun doing it.

## ADDITIONAL RESOURCES

Need some help planning a party? Check out Martha Stewart's Party Planning Checklist. http://images.marthastewart.com/images/content/web/pdfs/2009Q3/ms_checklist_partyplan.pdf

Want to host a wine tasting? Here's a link to a guide from *Food and Wine* magazine.
http://www.foodandwine.com/articles/how-to-host-a-wine-tasting

Ready to sponsor a bike ride for charity? Here's a link to a comprehensive checklist from ibike.org. http://www.ibike.org/encouragement/bike-a-thon.htm

*Lesson 34*

● ● ● ●

# YOU ARE A LEADER. BE MINDFUL OF THAT.

*You are not here merely to ... make a living. You are here in order to enable the world to live more amply, with greater vision, with a finer spirit of hope and achievement. You are here to enrich the world, and you impoverish yourself if you forget the errand.*

– WOODROW WILSON

## WOULD YOU WORK FOR YOUR FIRM?

I'm serious. Have you ever asked yourself that question? If you haven't, you should. Think about it for a moment. Have you created the kind of firm you'd choose to work for, or would be proud to have your kids work for? Are you the type of leader you want to be for your team and your community? Do you make a conscious effort to bring your best self to work each day? Do you walk into your office with a smile on your face? If you answered "Yes!" to these questions, congratulations! You can count yourself among the true legal elite. Whether you're leading a team of two, 10, 20, or just yourself, your leadership style affects everything about your law firm. If you answered "yes," read on to learn how you can get even better. If you answered "no" to one or two of the questions posed above, don't despair. Read on. There is one thing you can do that can change everything.

If there are things you'd like to change about how you lead, you can. In fact, there is one thing that you can do that will not only help you to improve your leadership, it will positively impact your general health, your ability to handle stress, and your ability to maintain your focus and attention. It costs you virtually nothing and can take a little as 10 minutes a day.

What is that one thing? Meditation – specifically, mindfulness meditation. If the idea of meditation freaks you out, relax. Literally. Mediation is not a religion, and it's not about spirituality, unless you want it to be. It's not about sitting cross-legged on the floor, unless that works for you. So what is it? Here's one of the best definitions I've found.

> Mindfulness is about observation without criticism; being compassionate with yourself. When unhappiness or stress hovers overhead, rather than taking it all personally, you learn to treat them as if they were black clouds in the sky, and to observe them with friendly curiosity as they drift past. In essence, mindfulness allows you to catch negative thought patterns before they tip you into a downward spiral. It begins the process of putting you back in control of your life.
> - From *Mindfulness: An Eight-Week Plan for Finding Peace in a Frantic World*,[34:1]

Meditation can reduce your stress and increase your focus. Meditation can boost your positivity, happiness, and feelings of well-being. Meditation can literally change your life. How? Through meditation you can change the neural pathways in your brain and break lifelong patterns of thinking and behavior. Neuroscience has discovered that our brains are constantly changing. Neuroplasticity is the term scientists use to express this concept. The neural pathways in our brains are not set during our childhood, as scientists during most of the 20th century believed. Rather, our brains are dynamic and capable of creating new neural pathways throughout our lives. And the most exciting aspect of this new neuroscience is that *we can affect these pathways.* We can create new pathways. Through meditation, we can use our mind to change our brain.

## YOUR BRAIN ON STRESS.

In the book, *Brain Rules: 12 Principles for Surviving and Thriving at Work, Home and School,*[34:2] author and molecular biologist John Medina explains that our brains are designed to deal with stress that lasts a very short time – seconds, in fact. When our ancestors faced stress from the fear of being eaten by a saber-toothed tiger, that stress came and went very quickly. You either ran away or were eaten – or maybe you killed the tiger. But it was all over very quickly. Today, our stressors last for days, weeks, months, or even longer. That is a big problem.

The two primary hormones that help us deal with stress – adrenaline and cortisol – are meant to defend us against acute stress – e.g., that saber-toothed tiger that wants to eat us.

> These days, our stresses are measured not in moments with mountain lions, but in hours, days, and sometimes months with hectic work-places, screaming toddlers, and money problems. Our system isn't built for that. And when moderate amounts of hormone build up to large amounts, or when moderate amounts of hormone hang around too long, they become quite harmful.
> - From *Brain Rules: 12 Principles for Surviving and Thriving at Work, Home and School*

The harmful effects of having stress hormones build up in our bodies over time can make us more susceptible to heart attacks and strokes. It can weaken our immune system and lessen our ability to fight infections. There are also tremendous negative effects of long-term stress on our brains. Our brains are very responsive to stress. If the stress is not too severe – good stress – our brains actually perform more effectively. (The theory that, when our stress level is just right, we perform at our best, is known as the Yerkes-Dodson Law.) But if our brains are subjected to chronic stress, the damage can be devastating. According to the research reported in *Brain Rules*, people affected by chronic stress don't process language efficiently, have poor long and short term memory, have poor concentration, and may suffer from depression.

> In almost every way it can be tested, chronic stress hurts our ability to learn. One study showed that adults with high stress levels performed 50 percent worse on certain cognitive tests than adults with low stress. Specifically, stress hurts declarative memory (things you can declare) and executive function (the type of thinking that involves problem-solving). Those, of course, are the skills needed to excel in school and business.
> - From *Brain Rules: 12 Principles for Surviving and Thriving at Work, Home, and School*

This is not good news for highly stressed lawyers. Living with high levels of chronic stress can negatively impact your health, your life, and your practice.

## MINDFULNESS AND LEADERSHIP

The book *Primal Leadership: Unleashing the Power of Emotional Intelligence*,[34:3] reports on the power of mindfulness, citing a study by the University of Wisconsin. In the study, University of Wisconsin researchers taught mindfulness meditation to scientists at a biotech firm who suffered from the stressful pace of their work. After just eight weeks in the study, the participants reported noticeably less stress – and they reported that they felt more creative and enthusiastic about their work. "But most remarkably, their brains had shifted toward less activity in the right prefrontal areas (which generate distressing emotions) and moved in the left— the brain's center for upbeat, optimistic feelings."

So what does this mean for you? Through mindfulness meditation, in as little as 10 minutes a day, you can begin to change the pathways in your brain to reduce your stress and create a positive impact on those around you. Numerous studies have found that people who meditate regularly are happier than the average person. But that's not all; a variety of other studies cited in *Mindfulness: An Eight –Week Plan for Finding Peace in a Frantic World* have found that:

* Anxiety, depression and irritability all decrease with regular sessions of meditation.
* Memory also improves, reaction times become faster, and mental and physical stamina increase.
* Regular meditators enjoy better and more fulfilling relationships.
* Studies worldwide have found that meditation reduces the key indicators of chronic stress, including hypertension.
* Meditation has also been found to be effective in reducing the impact of serious conditions, such as chronic pain and cancer, and can even help to relieve drug and alcohol dependence.
* Studies have now shown that meditation bolsters the immune system and thus helps to fight off colds, flu and other diseases.

Here's another great thing about mindfulness. It costs you practically nothing. All you need to do is get started. You may already be practicing a form of mindfulness through yoga or Tai Chi. If you are, then you know the benefits that being mindful can bring to every aspect of your life. I'm suggesting that you make time in your day to expand the practice. Even 10 minutes a day can make a big difference.

We often simply do not have the space, the breathing room, necessary to be clear and focused, and to listen deeply to ourselves and to others.
– From *Finding the Space to Lead: A Practical Guide to Mindful Leadership*[34:4]

## LIVING THE LESSON

I'd like to recommend three resources to get you started on your brain-changing journey. Each offers a different perspective on meditation and how it can have a positive impact on nearly every aspect of your life.

* *Meditations to Change Your Brain: Rewire Your Neural Pathways to Transform Your Life,*[34:5] by Rick Hanson, a neuropsychologist, and Rick Mendius, a board certified neurologist, is a fascinating look into how our brains work and what we can do to affect how our brains grow and change. *Meditations to Change Your Brain* is available only as an audio book or CD, as it contains numerous guided meditations. I suggest getting the Audible app for iPhone, Android or Windows Phone so that you can download the book directly to your phone. This audio book provides a tremendous amount of research about neuroplasticity and the value of meditation. It is excellent!

* Headspace.com is both a website and an app for your phone. The Headspace founder, Andy Puddicombe, has written the book on Headspace. Literally. His book, *Get Some Headspace: How Mindfulness Can Change Your Life in Ten Minutes a Day,*[34:6] is an excellent introduction to the practice of mindfulness. Headspace may be a crazy name, but the book, website, and app can change your life. I highly recommend reading the book, visiting the website, and downloading the app. The app and the first program, "Take 10," are free. Take 10 is a 10-day program of 10-minute guided meditations. If you're like me, you'll want more, and you can subscribe to the service which gives you access to all of the Headspace programs.

* Meditation Oasis provides a variety of guided meditations that are available through its app or as downloadable MP3 files. You can even go old school and purchase their guided meditations on CD. The meditations available on the app integrate your choice of background music or natural sounds, if you like. I have the app on my phone, and use it daily. The guided meditations in the "Relax & Rest" app help lull me off to a peaceful sleep nearly every night.

[34:1] Williams, Mark, and Penman, Danny (2011). *Mindfulness: An Eight-Week Plan for Finding Peace in a Frantic World.* Rodale.

[34:2] Medina, John (2010). *Brain Rules: 12 Principles for Surviving and Thriving at Work, Home and School.* Pear Press.

[34:3] Goleman, Daniel, Boyatzis, Richard, and McKee, Annie (2013). *Primal Leadership: Unleashing the Power of Emotional Intelligence.* Harvard Business School Publishing.

[34:4] Marturano, Janice (2014). *Finding the Space to Lead: A Practical Guide to Mindful Leadership.* Bloomsbury Press.

[34:5] Hanson, Rick and Mendius, Rick (2010). *Meditations to Change Your Brain: Rewire Your Neural Pathways to Transform Your Life.* Sounds True Publishing.

[34:6] Puddicombe, Andy (2011). *Get Some Headspace: How Mindfulness Can Change Your Life in Ten Minutes a Day.* Hodder & Stoughton.

*Lesson 35*

● ● ● ●

# LEARN HOW TO LISTEN. REALLY LISTEN.

*The greatest compliment that was ever paid me was when
one asked me what I thought, and attended to my answer.*

– HENRY DAVID THOREAU

Do you want to develop an extraordinary client base? "Of course I do," you're thinking. "What a silly question." Well then, I have four words for you: Learn how to listen. Learning to listen – really listen – is probably the single most significant thing you can do to improve your personal and professional relationships, and consequently improve your client base. Our lives are all about relationships. Not just our personal lives, but our professional lives, too. Relationships are about trust. Trust is built over time by truly understanding the other person. And the only way you can truly understand someone is to listen. Really listen.

Now, I have another question for you. Have you ever glanced at your email while talking with someone in your office? Or picked up your phone to check a text during a conversation? If you're honest, your answer to both questions is "yes." We've all done it at some point. In fact, we are so easily distracted by the buzz of our phones, that there is now a word to express how we feel when the person we're with pulls out their phone to answer a call or text. The word is "pizzled." Pizzled is a cross between pissed off and puzzled. Pizzled is not a good feeling. But most of us have felt pizzled at one time or another. And, unfortunately, most of us have been the "pizzler," not just the "pizzlee."

Nobody wants to feel pizzled. But I can almost guarantee you that you're working with a whole bunch of pizzled people. And it's not just you doing the pizzling. We've turned into a culture of pizzlers. In *The 7 Habits of Highly Effective People,*[35:1] Stephen Covey explains the importance of listening in the fifth habit: "Seek first to understand, then to be understood." The importance of listening lies at the core of being a great lawyer, a great leader, and a great person. Giving your undivided attention to another person demonstrates a very high level of respect. Conversely, when you fail to listen, you're demonstrating something very different. When you're not listening, you might as well be saying:

* You don't matter.
* I don't care about you.
* Your ideas don't matter.
* You're wrong.
* I don't understand you.
* I don't *want* to understand you.
* You're stupid.
* I'm stupid – for not giving you my attention.
* I'm too busy.
* You're wasting my time.

Listening – really listening – is crucial to your success as a lawyer. Not to mention, being a good listener won't hurt your personal life either. Your family and friends would like to have your attention when you're not at work. They'd like to be listened to just like your clients.

Unfortunately, "Listening 101" isn't taught in law school. So, if you want to be a better listener, listen up.

In *What Got You Here Won't Get You There,*[35:2] Marshall Goldsmith offers a list of listening tips. I've shared them here, tweaked just a bit for lawyers.

1. Don't interrupt. As much as you'd like to jump in and demonstrate that you understand what the other person is saying, don't do it.
2. Don't finish the other person's sentences. It doesn't matter if you know what the person is going to say; let them say it.
3. Don't say "I knew that." This is a tough one for lawyers.
4. Don't even agree with the other person. If he or she praises you, just say "Thank you."
5. Don't use the words "No," "But," and "However." When you use these words, you negate everything that comes before them in your conversation. Whenever you can, use the words "Yes, and…" or "Yes, and at the same time…" instead.
6. Don't be distracted. Give the person you're speaking with your full attention. Don't pizzle someone by pulling out your phone while you're having a conversation in your office. If you're in a social setting, DO NOT scan the room for "other" people to talk to while you're having a conversation.
7. Maintain your end of the conversation by asking intelligent questions that (a) show you're paying attention, (b) move the conversation forward, and (c) require the other person to talk (while you listen).
8. Eliminate any striving to impress the other person with how smart or how funny you are. Your only aim is to let the other person feel that *he or she* is accomplishing that.

I'll add two more tips to Goldsmith's that are listed above:

\* Don't think about how you're going to respond while you're listening. That's fine if you're listening to opposing counsel in a hearing. It's not okay when you're talking with anyone else. Your goal as a great listener should be to make the other person feel fantastic. If you truly listen, you will do just that.

* Don't attempt to multitask while someone is talking to you. The truth is you can't really multitask. (*See* Lesson 6. Understand and apply the power of focus.) Don't go through your mail, check your emails, glance at your project lists – you get the idea. Multitasking while someone is talking to you sends two very clear signals: 1) "What you are talking about is not important enough to really demand my attention." 2) Even if 1) is true, "I am rude."

In *What Got You Here Won't Get You There*, Goldsmith also sets forth a simple exercise to improve your listening skills: Count to 50. Focus on the counting and do your best not to let another thought creep into your mind. Maintain the count. Try it. How far did you get? This exercise demonstrates just how easily we can be distracted when we are not talking. It also helps develop your "concentration muscles" and your ability to focus. Do this exercise regularly until you can count to 50 without interrupting yourself. When you can do this, your listening skills will improve dramatically.

## LIVING THE LESSON

* All improvement starts with awareness. So, if you want to improve your listening skills, you can begin by simply noticing your listening habits. Do you engage in any of the behaviors outlined by Marshall Goldsmith? If you do, pick one, and commit to improving it.
* Ask someone who knows you well and whose opinion you trust if you engage in any of the negative listening behaviors listed above. Let them know you want to become a better listener and that their feedback will really help you. Then listen, and thank them for their feedback.
* Practice counting to 50. Do it once each day. Another powerful way to improve your focus, attention, and listening skills is to practice mindfulness. (*See* Lesson 34. You are a leader. Be mindful of that.)

[35:1] Covey, Stephen R. (1989, 2004). *The 7 Habits of Highly Effective People.* Simon & Schuster.
[35:2] Goldsmith, Marshall (2007). *What Got You Here Won't Get You There.* Hyperion.

*Lesson 36*

●  ●  ●  ●

# GET GOOD AT HANDLING CONFLICT.
# THINK CONSTRUCTIVE, NOT DESTRUCTIVE.

*Forces beyond your control can take away everything you possess except one thing, your freedom to choose how you will respond to the situation. You cannot control what happens to you in life, but you can always control what you will feel and do about what happens to you.*

— VIKTOR E. FRANKL

onflict. Just the mention of the word can conjure up any number of negative emotions and feelings for most people. Argue, fight, stress, anxiety, anger, frustration, and pain are but a few of the words that come to mind when people are asked what they think of when they hear the word "conflict."

While these emotions are no doubt a reality for many of us, conflict is a fact of life. Lawyers are in the business of conflict. Like it or not, we deal with conflict on a myriad of levels every day. Lawyers constantly face conflict situations with opposing counsel, colleagues, associates, team members and, yes, even with clients. The ability to deal constructively with conflict – regardless of where the conflict comes from – is an essential skill for all lawyers.

Although many negative reactions may be triggered by the idea of conflict, it is important to understand that conflict in and of itself is not negative. It is our response to conflict that can create a negative outcome.

Think about it. Every wonderful, exciting, beautiful thing in our world was born of, or is part of, conflict. Music is made up of the harmonization and dissonance of conflicting notes and patterns and rhythms. All sports are based on some type of conflict – whether in team competitions like football and basketball, or solo sports like tennis and golf. Great theater is great because of conflict. The movies let us experience conflict in thousands of different ways. If so many of the good things in life are born of and include conflict, why is our reaction to the idea of conflict so often negative?

While negative feelings toward conflict may indeed be common, a negative or destructive response will escalate the situation rather than diffuse it. How we choose to respond in any conflict situation can lead to either a successful outcome or a disaster. The key is how we choose to respond. The choice is ours, and we can choose to [READ: learn to] respond constructively.

Researchers at the Center for Conflict Dynamics at Eckerd College in St. Petersburg, Florida, have identified a number of responses to conflict – both constructive and destructive – that can serve to either minimize or escalate conflict. Many of us employ these responses or behaviors with little or no thought. Often our responses are simply habitual. We are often not consciously choosing how to respond to a given situation.

## CONSTRUCTIVE RESPONSES

Research has shown that the kinds of constructive behaviors listed below are highly effective in keeping the harmful effects of conflict to a minimum. Constructive responses emphasize:

*   Creative problem-solving
*   A focus on the exchange of ideas
*   Expression of positive emotions and optimism
*   Not provoking the other person

If your typical response to conflict is constructive, that's great. Regardless of the type of conflict – in the office with team members, with opposing counsel, or even with clients – constructive responses will lead to better outcomes. If you find that you don't usually respond constructively to conflict, you're probably used to being in the middle of some very rocky situations. The important thing to understand is that responding constructively is a skill that can be learned. It starts with self-awareness, knowing your habitual responses and making a conscious effort to change them. It's important to keep in mind that improving your constructive responses even slightly will pay big dividends.

Even if you're not employing constructive responses as often as you could, the constructive responses listed may seem familiar to you. You may have heard of some of them, or it may seem like common sense that these types of responses might be an optimal way to respond to conflict. In fact, research has shown that the more we use these constructive responses, the more positive our conflict outcomes will be. The challenge is to actually use these responses, as opposed to responding as we habitually do, especially if our habitualized responses are destructive.

*Words, like eyeglasses, blur everything they do not make clear.*

*– JOSEPH JOUBERT*

## DESTRUCTIVE RESPONSES

Research has shown that the kinds of behaviors listed below will tend to escalate or prolong conflict. Destructive responses emphasize:

* * Displaying negative emotions
* * Trying to win, no matter what
* * Lack of respect for the other person
* * Avoiding conflict rather than facing it

We've all been on the receiving end of destructive responses to conflict. Some people use only destructive responses when faced with conflict. The challenge for lawyers is to not confuse advocacy with utilizing destructive responses. In the heat of battle, it can be difficult to pause long enough to choose the appropriate response to the situation; but the more you can begin to do just that, the more effective you'll be, both in the courtroom, and in every other aspect of your life.

> *First keep the peace within yourself, then*
> *you can also bring peace to others.*
>
> — THOMAS À KEMPIS

## KNOW YOUR HOT BUTTONS

Conflict research has found that there are certain situations and behaviors that irritate us. Those situations are our hot buttons. When someone pushes our hot buttons, we are more likely to use destructive behaviors in response. At one time or another, you've probably said (through gritted teeth), "He sure knows how to push my buttons!" Sometimes, just the mere thought of a person or situation can push one of your hot buttons, aggravate you, and make you more likely to react destructively. When I practiced law, there was one attorney in particular who pushed all of my hot buttons. He was a bully, and just hearing that he was on the phone caused my blood pressure to rise. Then one day, I read the quote from Viktor Frankl at the beginning of this lesson, and it was like a light bulb went off in my head. I didn't have to give this guy that kind of power over me! I could choose how I was going to respond to him. It didn't matter what he said or what he did or how aggravated or irritated I was. I could react constructively. The added bonus for reacting constructively to bullies is that it throws them off their game. They behave in a certain way so that you'll respond in the way they want you to. When you don't, you have more control over the situation and can move it forward constructively.

## THE NINE HOT BUTTONS

In their book, *Becoming a Conflict Competent Leader*,[36:1] authors Craig Runde and Tim Flanagan identify nine hot button behaviors that can trigger conflict and, at the same time, make us more susceptible to using destructive behaviors in response. Although there are any number of behaviors that can irritate people, Runde and Flanagan found these nine to be most prevalent in workplace settings:

1. Abrasiveness: Arrogant, sarcastic and demeaning
2. Aloofness: Isolating, not seeking input, hard to approach
3. Hostility: Angry, yelling, losing temper
4. Micromanagement: Constantly monitoring and checking on others
5. Overly analytical: Focusing on minor issues; perfectionism
6. Self-centered: Caring only about self, believing they are always correct
7. Lack of appreciation: Failing to give credit, seldom praising good performance
8. Unreliability: Missing deadlines, cannot be counted on
9. Lack of trustworthiness: Exploiting others, taking undeserved credit

Knowing what your hottest hot buttons are can help you begin to learn to respond to them more constructively. Runde and Flanagan suggest a three-step approach when responding to conflict:

1. Cool down: Cooling down requires the ability to manage our emotions. First, by recognizing that our hot button has been pushed, we can pause, or take a breath, or count to 10 – whatever works for you.
2. Slow down: When emotions are running so high that your cool-down strategy isn't working, it's time to slow down. In the book *Getting to Yes*,[36:2] Roger Fisher and William Ury speak about "going to the balcony." Take a time out – literally and figuratively. Step back from the situation, and view it from the balcony, as though you were watching a play unfold before you. Don't return to the conversation until you're ready for step three.
3. Engage constructively: Once you have cooled down and slowed down so that you are in control of your emotions, you'll be able to engage with the other person, using constructive behaviors.

In the heat of conflict, it can be difficult to remember to slow down or to find a good way to ask for a time-out. So we recommend developing plans in advance for what to do when things are racing in the wrong direction.

– From *Building Conflict Competent Teams*[36:3]


## LIVING THE LESSON

* Take a minute and ask yourself these questions:
  o How often do I face conflict in the workplace?
  o When conflict occurs, do I prefer to avoid dealing with it or give in to others?
  o Do I come off too aggressively at times?
  o Do I take time to listen to other people's thoughts on an issue?
  o When conflicts emerge, am I aware of my feelings and those of others?
  o Do I rush to solve problems before I'm sure of what the issues are?
  o Do I collaborate with others to come up with solutions, or do I make most of the decisions on my own?
* What do your answers tell you about how you approach conflict?
* Do you respond more frequently with constructive or destructive behaviors? If you find that you're more likely to use destructive responses to conflict, use the "cool down, slow down, engage constructively" model to begin to develop your constructive response skills.
* Visit the Center for Conflict Dynamics at Eckerd College and find out what your hottest hot button is: http://www.conflictdynamics.org/products/cdp/hb/

[36:1] Flanagan, Tim A., and Runde, Craig E. (2007). *Becoming a Conflict Competent Leader*. Jossey-Bass.

[36:2] Fisher, Roger, and Ury, William (2011). *Getting to Yes: Negotiating Agreement Without Giving In.* Penguin Books.

[36:3] Flanagan, Tim A., and Runde, Craig E. (2008). *Building Conflict Competent Teams.* Jossey-Bass.

## ADDITIONAL RESOURCES

*Becoming a Resonant Leader*, by Richard Boyatzis, Frances Johnston, and Annie McKee.

*Man's Search for Meaning*, by Viktor E. Frankl.

*Lesson 37*

●　　●　　●　　●

## SAY "I'M SORRY" WHEN YOU MAKE A MISTAKE.

*An apology is a lovely perfume; it can transform
the clumsiest moment into a gracious gift.*

— MARGARET LEE RUNBECK

Have you ever seen the movie *Love Story*? If not, you've probably heard the famous line from the 1970 tearjerker. If you've seen the movie, you'll remember Jennifer Cavalleri's famous line to Oliver Barrett. They'd had an argument. Oliver ran out. He came back to find Jenny crying on the steps of their apartment. As he began to say he was sorry, Jenny interrupted him and said…wait for it…"Love means never having to say you're sorry." Well, what may be true for love [really?], isn't true for leadership. Saying you're sorry – and meaning it – shows that you care about the relationship. Oh, and it shows that you're not a jerk. Leaders understand the importance of acknowledging and apologizing for their mistakes.

In his book, *What Got You Here Won't Get You There,*[37:1] Marshall Goldsmith identifies 20 habits that hold leaders back. Habit #15 is "Refusing to express regret: The inability to take responsibility for our actions, admit we're wrong, or recognize how our actions affect others." All too often we get caught up in wanting to be right, and we think of apologizing as a sign of weakness. But nothing could be further from the truth. Refusing to say "I'm sorry," when you've screwed up actually says something else. It says you really don't care about the people around you.

> Apologizing is one of the most powerful and resonant gestures in the human arsenal – almost as powerful as a declaration of love. It's "I love you" flipped on its head. If love means, "I care about you and I'm happy about it," then an apology means, "I hurt you and I'm sorry about it." Either way, it's seductive and irresistible; it irrevocably changes the relationship between two people. It compels them to move forward into something new and, perhaps, wonderful together.
>
> - From *What Got You Here Won't Get You There*

By making a habit of expressing sincere and specific appreciation for the work your people do and apologizing when you screw up, you'll begin nurturing a solid team of engaged employees. (For more on the importance of engaged employees, *see* Lesson 46. Say "thank you" every day, and mean it.)

Here's another bonus to saying you're sorry when you make a mistake: You demonstrate to everyone on your team that it's okay to make a mistake as long as you own up to it. Most mistakes – even mistakes in a law firm – can be fixed, IF you know about them when they happen. By apologizing, you're creating a culture that says it's okay to make mistakes if you don't try to cover them up. Admitting our mistakes is the first step toward fixing them when they happen.

## LIVING THE LESSON

* Learn how to apologize. Keep it simple. Ready? Here's exactly what you say: "I'm sorry." And, as Goldsmith points out, you can add: "I'll try to do better in the future." That way, you're acknowledging that

you've made a mistake, AND you're making a conscious effort to change your behavior.

[37:1] Goldsmith, Marshall (2007). *What Got You Here Won't Get You There.* Hyperion.

*Lesson 38*

●　●　●　●

# INNOVATION OR CONTINUOUS IMPROVEMENT? YES.

*The best way to predict the future is to invent it.*

— ALAN KAY

The practice of law is not what it was 10 years ago, or five years ago, or even three years ago. Pressure from an ever-changing economy, the commoditization of legal services from companies like LegalZoom, the phenomenal pace of technology, and the never-ending search for more work-life balance and more profits compel radical changes in how law firms are structured and run. Law firms that want to do more than merely survive in the years ahead must reevaluate how they operate.

There is strong evidence that unprecedented changes in practice are producing a restructuring in the way legal services are delivered. These changes include widespread access to legal information, the routinization of many legal tasks, demands by clients for more control of legal service delivery, and the emergence of an increasingly competitive marketplace. This restructuring in the way legal services are delivered affects all law firms – regardless of size, geographic location, and substantive practice area – although it may impact different firms in different ways. Clients are seeking more efficient services, predictable fees, and increased responsiveness to their needs, and they are willing to replace their lawyers if they are not satisfied with the services they receive.

- From *The New York State Bar Association: Report of the Task Force on the Future of the Legal Profession, February 2011*

Despite the realities of the evolving legal landscape, most lawyers remain very resistant to change. YOU are not most lawyers. You know that the practice and business of law must change, and you must change with it. So the question becomes: How? Does the answer lie in the concept of innovation – swift, dramatic, sweeping change, or in continuous improvement – small steps over time? The truth is – the answer lies in a combination of both approaches. In order to thrive in the years ahead, the best lawyers and law firms will embrace both innovation AND continuous improvement.

The New York State bar Association Report underscores the need for innovation and continuous improvement in law. While neither concept is a panacea, successful law firms cannot ignore either of these approaches to change. Opportunities for innovation and continuous improvement are everywhere. You need only take a look around your office to see them.

## THE CASE FOR INNOVATION

*Innovation is the ability to convert ideas into invoices.*

*– L. DUNCAN*

Innovation is about big change – massive change. Completely rethinking how a service is provided or how clients pay for the services you provide are fertile grounds for innovation. And depending upon your practice area and the work you do, innovation in these areas may be absolutely necessary.

In Gary Hamel's book, *What Matters Now: How to Win in a World of Relentless Change, Ferocious Competition, and Unstoppable Innovation,*[38:1] Hamel talks about the importance of innovation in a rapidly changing world. Hamel has long been a thought leader in the area of innovation, and his call to innovation should resonate with all lawyers. Innovation is about big change, and the legal profession could benefit from some big changes. Today's law firm is built on a model created more than 100 years ago. How many businesses could exist today in a model that has barely changed in more than 100 years? The bottom line: Law firms that refuse to innovate – at least on some levels – will not be able to compete in the 21st century.

> In recent years, left-brain types have had the upper hand while starry-eyed innovators have struggled to get a hearing. Nevertheless, before innovation slips any further down the list of corporate priorities, we need to remind ourselves that we owe everything to innovation.
> – From *What Matters Now: How to Win in a World of Relentless Change, Ferocious Competition, and Unstoppable Innovation*

Did you hear that, left-brainers? Law firms aren't known for their willingness to embrace innovation. But ignore innovation at your peril. So, what exactly are we talking about when we use the word innovation? In a law firm, innovation can mean any number of things. Here are just a few areas that are ripe for innovation in most law firms:

* Re-examining how you deliver your services
* Considering value pricing or alternative fee agreements
* Providing flex-time to employees, or allowing them to work virtually
* Expanding your core competencies around business and leadership
* Leveraging cloud-based case management or other services

This list may not sound earth-shattering, but there are far too many law firms that don't embrace any of these ideas. They'll say, "We don't have the time." "We tried it before, and it didn't' work." "We don't have the resources."

"Nobody else is doing that." "We're doing fine just as we are." Do any of these comments sound familiar to you?

So why does innovation matter? Innovation matters because if you're not innovating, you're being commoditized. Innovation matters because law firms that don't innovate will lose clients to the firms that do, *or* to online legal service providers (THINK: LegalZoom and RocketLawyer). Innovation matters because law firms that continue to innovate will distinguish themselves from companies that provide legal services online.

What are you doing to move your practice and your life in the direction you want to go? Have you stepped out of line recently? Have you challenged what you accept as true for you? Have you thought about just one innovation that could dramatically improve your law practice? If not, why not?

> For every nine people who denounce innovation, only one will encourage it. … For every nine people who do things the way they have always been done, only one will ever wonder if there is a better way. For every nine people who stand in line in the front of a locked building, only one will ever come around and check the back door. Our progress as a species rests squarely on the shoulders of that tenth person. The nine are satisfied with the things they are told are valuable. Person 10 determines for himself what has value.
> – From *The Backdoor to Enlightenment* [38:2]

## A KAIZEN MINDSET

*Sustained success is largely a matter of focusing regularly on the right things and making a lot of uncelebrated little improvements every day.*

*— THEODORE LEVITT*

Unlike the massive change that innovation brings, Kaizen, or continuous improvement, works on a distinctly different level. The word Kaizen is a Japanese word meaning "good change" or "change for the best." Kaizen is about creating a culture of continuous improvement. A Kaizen culture of continuous improvement relies on small, incremental steps that, over time, produce big results.

Innovation and Kaizen together are a potent combination for creating lasting, positive change for your firm. Kaizen's small steps can provide the perfect introduction to change within your firm. Kaizen's culture of small step, continuous improvement works very differently than innovative approaches. And in some situations, Kaizen can be even more effective. Think about your own life. Let's talk about the "I'm going to get in shape and go to the gym every morning at 6 a.m." innovation. Is there anyone who hasn't tried implementing that innovation? If you're one of the lucky ones, maybe it worked for you. But if you're like millions of other people, you probably made it to the gym for a day or two and then found plenty of reasons why that innovation was just not going to work.

If you were to approach getting in shape with a Kaizen mindset, you'd ask yourself the question, "What is one small thing I could do every day that would help me become healthier?" Maybe the answer is to take a 20-minute walk – every day. That walk becomes part of your life, just like brushing your teeth in the morning. Over time, that one small step can improve your health dramatically.

The reason that Kaizen is so effective is that its small changes often don't really feel like changes at all. They are slight, sometimes almost imperceptible. But like the effect of water dripping on a rock, they will change the landscape of your world over time.

## LIVING THE LESSON

* Innovation: Identify one process or system in your office to innovate. Think big, dramatic change! What is one BIG change that you could make that would improve the service you provide to your clients? Identify it and do it.
* Kaizen: Look for ways to make very small changes. Ask these questions of yourself and your team:

- o What is one thing we could do to save us a few dollars each day?
- o Is there a small change we could make that would improve our clients' experiences?
- o Is there one thing we could do each day, that wouldn't cost any money, but would reduce waste in the office?
- \* Get in the habit of always asking the question: "Is there a better way?"

[38:1] Hamel, Gary (2012). *What Matters Now: How to Win in a World of Relentless Change, Ferocious Competition, and Unstoppable Innovation.* Jossey-Bass.

[38:2] Nebeisieck, Ashley, and Rinpoche, Za (2007). *The Backdoor to Enlightenment.* Three Leaves Press.

*Lesson 39*

●　　●　　●　　●

# WORDS MATTER. THEY CREATE YOUR LIFE.

*The word is not just a sound or a written symbol. The word is
a force; it is the power you have to express and communicate,
to think, and thereby to create the events in your life.*

– DON MIGUEL RUIZ, THE FOUR AGREEMENTS

As a lawyer, words are your stock in trade. You use them to craft just the right phrase in a contract. You speak them to argue on your client's behalf. You negotiate with them. Sometimes you may even yell them at the people in your office.

Words matter. Just as you must learn how to listen effectively (*see* Lesson 35. Learn how to listen. Really Listen.), you must also learn to use your words effectively. This goes beyond your work as a lawyer. It is your responsibility as a human being. In *The Four Agreements*,[39:1] Don Miguel Ruiz speaks to the importance of being "impeccable with your word." Words are double-edged swords, so we must be mindful of how we use them. Your words can create understanding and resonance – or they can create frustration, anger, and dissonance. It's your choice, so choose wisely.

## HOW WE TALK TO OTHERS

The words we speak to others don't affect only the people with whom we are speaking. Our words create a ripple effect. Like a stone thrown into a still pond, our words create ripples that can reach far beyond the original conversation. The effect of negative words on someone in your office can linger long after the workday is over. Haven't we all experienced situations where the words spoken to us played over and over in our heads? "What he said got me so upset I couldn't get to sleep last night!" "I can't stop thinking about how she criticized my work this morning." Your words have power.

*Once a word has been allowed to escape, it cannot be recalled.*

*— HORACE*

But there is equal power in positive words. Look for ways to use positive language whenever you can. Your "positive" ripples will also last long after the workday is over. The next time you are tempted to use negative words in your office, stop and think about who else may be impacted by your words. A husband? A wife? A child? Use your words to create ripples of positivity for the people you work with and everyone else in their lives.

*A word is not a crystal, transparent and unchanged;*
*it is the skin of a living thought, and may vary*
*greatly in color and content according to the*
*circumstances and the time in which it is used.*

*— OLIVER WENDELL HOLMES*

## HOW WE TALK TO OURSELVES

It's not an easy task to be impeccable with your word in conversations with others. And it may be even more challenging to be impeccable with your word when you talk to yourself. Make no mistake: You talk to yourself all the time. And if the majority of your self-talk is negative, you're not alone. Everyone has a negative voice in their heads at least some of the time. Some examples of negative self-talk include: "I'll never get all this work done." "I hate marketing." "I'm never going to have enough clients." "There just isn't enough time in the day."

Our self-talk usually centers around worries and problems, and we can really beat ourselves up. This negative self-talk may be due – at least in part – to how our brains work. We can conjure up worries and problems and talk to ourselves incessantly about them, using very little energy. But focusing on our goals instead of worries, or focusing on solutions instead of problems, takes much more brain power. It's how we're wired. In *Your Brain at Work*,[39:2] author David Rock explains that we spend more time focused on problems (things we've seen) than solutions (things we've not seen) because it's harder for us to envision the future. As a result, we end up constantly talking to ourselves about our problems and worries.

But just as you can make a conscious effort when choosing the words you speak to others, you can make the same conscious effort with respect to the words you speak to yourself. Would you let a friend talk to you the way YOU talk to you?! If your answer is NO, then begin noticing when you're beating yourself up. Choose your words – including the words in your own head – wisely.

The human mind is like a fertile ground where seeds are continually being planted. The seeds are opinions, ideas, and concepts. You plant a seed, a thought, and it grows. The word is like a seed, and the human mind is so fertile! The only problem is that too often it is fertile for the seeds of fear. Every human mind is fertile, but only for those kinds of seeds it is prepared for. What is important is to see which kind of seeds our mind is fertile for, and to prepare it to receive the seeds of love.

- From *The Four Agreements: A Practical Guide to Personal Freedom (A Toltec Wisdom Book)*

## LIVING THE LESSON

*   Think before you speak. Your words have a ripple effect on people you may never know.
*   Look for opportunities to brighten someone's day with a kind word.
*   Watch your self-talk. Notice when your self-talk is negative, and replace negative talk with more positive words.

[39:1] Ruiz, Don Miguel (2007). *The Four Agreements: A Practical Guide to Personal Freedom (A Toltec Wisdom Book)*. Amber-Allen Publishing.
[39:2] Rock, David (2009). *Your Brain at Work: Strategies for Overcoming Distraction, Regaining Focus, and Working Smarter All Day Long*. HarperBusiness.

## ADDITIONAL RESOURCES

*The Success Principles: How to Get From Where You Are to Where You Want to Be*, by Jack Canfield
*Mindfulness: An Eight –Week Plan for Finding Peace in a Frantic World*, by Mark Williams and Danny Penman

*Lesson 40*

●　●　●　●

# GET TO KNOW YOURSELF.

*He who knows others is wise. He who
knows himself is enlightened.*

*– LAO TZU*

In Hamlet, Polonius prepares his son, Laertes, for travel with the following advice: "This above all: To thine own self be true." Unless you can first be true to yourself, you cannot be true to others. Successful people follow Polonius' advice, although it is no easy task. To be true to yourself means you must first know yourself. To know yourself, you must first be self-aware. To be self-aware we must understand ourselves – and understand how we are perceived by others.

Why is self-awareness important? Because without self-awareness, we can get caught up in behaviors that are inconsistent with our own values and beliefs. Without self-awareness, we may not have the courage to say "no" to the unimportant things in life so that we can focus on the truly important. Without self-awareness, we may fear appearing vulnerable. Without self-awareness, we can't understand how our characteristics and behaviors are impacting other people. Self-awareness gives us the ability to utilize our behaviors and characteristics in ways that serve us best.

In her book, *Lawyer, Know Thyself: A Psychological Analysis of Personality Strengths and Weaknesses,* [40:1] Susan Swaim Daicoff explains that some of the very characteristics that make lawyers successful in the courtroom can lead to problems in more collaborative environments and in their everyday lives.

> For example, being a predominantly rational, objective, competitive and argumentative sort of person may allow one to function well as an advocate during the workday, but be quite destructive to one's interpersonal relationships. It may bleed over into being hostile, argumentative, and aggressive in all situations, which could hamper one's ability to relate well with others, and thus impair one's ability to garner social and collegial support.
>
> - From *Lawyer, Know Thyself*

In other words, when you're meeting with the team in your office, remember, it's not an adversarial contest. If you lack self-awareness, you may not realize that the characteristics that serve you well in the courtroom may not serve you well as a leader in your own firm. Ironically, you may notice these adversarial characteristics in your colleagues, yet not be aware of them in yourself.

All too often, behavior we dislike in others – behavior that drives us crazy – is the very behavior we sometimes exhibit. And while we may refuse to recognize our own problem behaviors, they may be very obvious to those around us.

> *Everything that irritates us about others can*
> *lead us to an understanding of ourselves.*
>
> — *CARL JUNG*

If we can stop, listen, and think about what others are seeing in us, we have a great opportunity. We can compare the self that we want to be with the self that we are presenting to the world. We can then begin to make the real changes that are needed to close the gap that sometimes exists between our values and how we actually behave.

## SELF-AWARENESS LEADS TO INTEGRATION, NOT DISINTEGRATION

Much of the stress so many attorneys feel in their day-to-day practice stems from what Steven Keeva refers to as disintegration. In his classic *Transforming Practices: Finding Joy and Satisfaction in the Legal Life*,[40:2] Keeva explains the importance of integrating your heart and mind into your law practice. Written in 1999, *Transforming Practices* was ahead of its time and speaks to the hunger for integration expressed by so many lawyers today.

> It isn't easy to pin down what it means to be whole or integrated. But it's worth trying. Here are some qualities or experiences that may give at least a hint of what the desired state is all about:
>
> * You have a sense of diversity in your life – diversity of feelings, thoughts, and experiences. In social and biological systems, diversity is a sign of strength and vibrancy. So it is in individuals, who atrophy when they become emotionally and intellectually monochromatic. Great strength, and a sense of harmony, comes from the unfettered interplay of intellect, spirit, and emotions.
> * You are able to articulate, to your own satisfaction, what matters to you and what principles guide you in your life. You live in harmony with them, both at work and at home.
> * You see your work as a servant of your values, passions, and sense of purpose in life.
> * You are emotionally open and – at least in some circumstances – able to laugh with gusto, to cry, to be real.
> * When you are angry, you are aware of it and you take responsibility for it, rather than making it someone else's fault.
>
> - From *Transforming Practices Finding Joy and Satisfaction in the Legal Life*

The key to creating a law practice that serves your life – instead of living a life that serves your law practice – is to integrate your practice with your life. The path to integration is different for every lawyer, and *Transforming Practices* sets forth seven different approaches to integration. But while the path to integration is different for each person, according to Keeva, the signs of disintegration are universal and include:

* Feeling like a stranger to yourself
* Feeling like your life is living you, rather than vice versa
* Not really feeling aware of what's going on around you
* Feeling as if your life is out of your control
* Rarely, if ever, taking time to reflect on life's big questions
* Exhibiting some type of obsessive behavior

If you recognize any of these signs, you may want to create a new way of practicing law for yourself. By creating a meaningful inner life, you will nourish your professional life, so that what you do becomes more of an expression of who you are.

While such thinking may seem "new age" and "too touchy feely" for many attorneys, consider this. Oliver Wendell Holmes gave similar advice many years ago in a letter to a young man just starting his legal career. In *A Nation Under Lawyers: How the Crisis in the Legal Profession is Transforming American Society*,[40:3] author Mary Ann Glendon tells the story of a young lawyer, Charlie Wyzanski, who in 1927 wrote to then Supreme Court Justice Holmes, and asked, "What do you have to say to someone embarking on a legal career?" Justice Holmes' advice is just as relevant today as it was in 1927. Here is an excerpt from Justice Holmes' response, "For your sake I hope that when your work seems to present only mean details you may realize that every detail has the mystery of the universe behind it and may keep up your heart with an undying faith."

## LIVING THE LESSON

* Give yourself time to think deeply about your life and your practice.
* Keep a journal of the things you really enjoy doing and when you're feeling your best during the day.

*   If this lesson has resonated with you, read *Transforming Practices* for more insights and approaches to creating a more balanced, integrated life.

[40:1] Swaim Daicoff, Susan (2004). *Lawyer, Know Thyself: A Psychological Analysis of Personality Strengths and Weaknesses.* American Psychological Association.

[40:2] Keeva, Steven (1999). *Transforming Practices: Finding Joy and Satisfaction in the Legal Life.* American Bar Association.

[40:3] Glendon, Mary Ann (1994). *A Nation Under Lawyers: How the Crisis in the Legal Profession is Transforming American Society.* Harvard University Press.

## ADDITIONAL RESOURCES

*Anyway: The Paradoxical Commandments – Finding Personal Meaning in a Crazy World*, by Kent M. Keith.

*The Art of Possibility: Transforming Professional and Personal Life*, by Rosamund Stone Zander and Benjamin Zander.

*Lesson 41*

● ● ● ●

# CHECK YOUR ATTITUDE AT THE DOOR.

*If you can't laugh, smile. If you can't smile, grin. If
you can't grin, stay out of the way until you can.*

— WINSTON CHURCHILL

How do you feel when you walk through the front door of your office? I bet you're thinking, "How can I answer that question? Every time is different. It depends on where I'm coming from – literally and figuratively." While that may be true, it's your responsibility to be aware of your mood every time you walk into your office. Whatever your mood and attitude may be, good or bad, it's your choice. And your attitude affects every single person in your office. If you're in a good mood, everyone around you picks up on it. They can't help it. The same is true for our bad moods. Our emotions are contagious.

Think about it for a minute. Have you ever started laughing just because you heard someone else laughing? Have your eyes filled with tears at the sight of another person crying? Have you ever yawned in response to seeing a tired friend yawn? Are you yawning now, just thinking about yawning? If you answered "yes" to any of these questions, you've experienced the contagiousness of our moods.

Contagious good moods can boost morale and productivity. Bad moods are contagious, too, and can infect everyone in the office, causing morale and productivity to plummet.

> The Law of Leadership Modeling states that the positive things you do in excess, followers will do in moderation. But the negative things you do in moderation, they will emulate in excess.
> -From *Up Your Business! 7 Steps to Fix, Build, or Stretch Your Organization*[41:1]

## RESONANT V. DISSONANT LEADERSHIP – A BIT OF SCIENCE

In the book *Primal Leadership: Unleashing the Power of Emotional Intelligence,*[41:2] authors Daniel Goleman, Richard Boyatzis and Annie McKee explain how the leader's mood creates either a productive (resonant) or toxic (dissonant) work environment. It all starts with our limbic system and something scientists call "the open loop."

> Scientists describe the open loop as "interpersonal limbic regulation," whereby one person transmits signals that can alter hormone levels, cardiovascular function, sleep rhythms, and even immune function inside the body of another. That's how couples who are in love are able to trigger in one another's brains surges of oxytocin, which creates a pleasant, affectionate feeling. But in all aspects of social life, not just love relationships, our physiologies intermingle, our emotions automatically shifting into the register of the person we're with. The open-loop design of the limbic system means that other people can change our very physiology – and so our emotions.
> - From *Primal Leadership*

People around you pick up on your mood, and will mirror that mood. When you are positive, warm and upbeat, you send out emotions that create a resonant climate in your office. You can feel the energy and enthusiasm of a resonant climate. It is a place where people enjoy working, where they feel valued, and consequently are happier and more productive. When you are negative, cold, and irritable, you send out emotions that create a dissonant climate. We've all been in a dissonant working climate at some point in our lives. No one enjoys working in a dissonant environment. We know what it feels like, and it doesn't feel good. A dissonant climate is one filled with tension, discord, and toxicity. The people don't want to be there, and as a result, they are much less productive than people who work in a resonant climate and for a resonant leader.

*Laughter is the shortest distance between two people.*

— VICTOR BORGE

Now, I'm not saying that resonance means that there are never any problems or tensions in an office. There will always be pressures and deadlines in a law office, and a certain level of stress can be a good thing. But prolonged, unrelenting stress and negativity diminishes our brain's capacity to process information and dramatically reduces our productivity. According to *Primal Leadership*, "A good laugh or an upbeat mood, on the other hand, more often enhances the neural abilities crucial for doing good work."

*If you cannot smile, do not open a shop.*

— CHINESE PROVERB

In order to be truly effective, you've got to get good at controlling your emotions and attitudes. Here's the good news: You can make a conscious decision to change your attitude at any time. As a leader in your firm, it's your job to model the kinds of attitudes and behaviors you want to encourage in your team. Before you step into your next meeting or walk through the door of your office, check your attitude. Are you relaxed or are you stressed out? Are you tight-lipped because you're still irritated by that last phone call with opposing counsel, or are you ready to smile – genuinely smile? Are you already smiling? If you're angry, frustrated, or just in a bad mood, pause for a moment as you reach for the door. In this moment, you can choose to change your attitude. I'm not saying that it's easy to do, but I am saying that you must get in the habit of doing it. Otherwise, you will always be at the mercy of your own emotions, rather than being in control of them. And if your emotions are negative, everyone in your office will "catch" them.

> *Between stimulus and response there is a space. In*
> *that space is our power to choose our response. In*
> *our response lies our growth and our freedom.*
>
> – *Viktor E. Frankl*

Lawyers must also be able to check their "lawyerly" thinking at the door. You know the old saying, "Law school teaches you to think like a lawyer." I've never met an attorney who's told me, "You know, I was so cynical and pessimistic before I became a lawyer, but law school sure changed all that!" While the critical thinking skills that law school teaches are invaluable to your role as an advocate, they can create challenges for you in other aspects of your life. Self-awareness is key. (*See* Lesson 40. Get to know yourself.) The ability to think critically about a situation without being cynical or negative is an essential trait of good leadership. Leaders know how to ask the right questions with the right attitude. Their questions are not designed to intimidate or dominate or put people on the spot. Rather, their questions are designed to help them to learn, or to delegate better, or to acknowledge others, or to enhance communication.

Consider the climate in your office; is it positive or negative? Whatever the climate, environment, or mood, it is a reflection of YOU. You are being watched all the time, and your mood is highly contagious. You set the tone for your office. So, make a conscious choice to set a resonant tone, not a dissonant one.

> *The longer I live, the more I realize the impact of attitude*
> *on life. Attitude, to me, is more important than facts. It is*

*more important than the past, than education, than money,
than circumstances, than failures, than successes, than what
other people think or say or do. It is more important than
appearance, giftedness or skill. It will make or break a
company...a church...a home. The remarkable thing is we
have a choice everyday regarding the attitude we will embrace
for that day. We cannot change our past...we cannot change
the fact that people will act in a certain way. We cannot change
the inevitable. The only thing we can do is play on the one
string we have, and that is our attitude. I am convinced that
life is 10% what happens to me and 90% how I react to it.
And so it is with you...we are in charge of our attitudes.*

— *Charles Swindoll*

## LIVING THE LESSON

* Notice. Just begin to notice your moods.
* Check your attitude – not just at the door – but throughout the day. Are you sending out upbeat, positive emotions and creating a resonant climate? Or, are you sending out negative emotions that create a dissonant climate?
* Train your brain to be more positive. You may think this is impossible, but it's not. You can use "mindfulness," to literally grow your brain's capacity for upbeat, optimistic feelings. (*See* Lesson 34. You are a leader. Be mindful of that).

[41:1] Anderson, Dave (2003). *Up Your Business! 7 Steps to Fix, Build, or Stretch Your Organization*. John Wiley & Sons, Inc.
[41:2] Goleman, Daniel, Boyatzis, Richard, and McKee, Annie (2013). *Primal Leadership: Unleashing the Power of Emotional Intelligence*. Harvard Business Review Press.

## Lesson 42

•  •  •  •

# WHEN HIRING, EXPERIENCE MATTERS. BUT NOT SO MUCH.

*Hire and promote first on the basis of integrity; second,
motivation; third, capacity; fourth, understanding; fifth,
knowledge; and last and least, experience. Without integrity,
motivation is dangerous; without motivation, capacity
is impotent; without capacity, understanding is limited;
without understanding, knowledge is meaningless; without
knowledge, experience is blind. Experience is easy to provide
and quickly put to use by people with all the other qualities.*

— DEE HOCK, FOUNDER AND CEO EMERITUS OF VISA

Have you ever had any "people" problems in your firm? If you're like most lawyers, the answer is a resounding "yes." Who hasn't had to deal with personnel issues in their law firm? Nobody. And if you're like many lawyers, you'd rather be grilled before the Supreme Court than address people problems in your own office.

Have you ever noticed that very often (most of the time?) people problems have nothing to do with skill or experience? Don't get me wrong – skill and experience do matter. But they shouldn't be the first qualities you look for when hiring. In fact, they should be pretty far down the list. Let me be clear: I'm not saying that *competence* doesn't matter. Your people must be competent. Competence and experience are two very different things. If you hire competent people, regardless of experience, you can give them the experience YOU want them to have. Have you ever hired someone with considerable experience, and found out it was the wrong kind of experience? Experience that taught them it was okay to cut corners or not really care about the clients they serve?

All the experience in the world won't make up for a lack of integrity, shared values, or cultural fit. You know what I'm talking about. When you have someone on your staff who lacks integrity or doesn't share your firm's values, it will make you and everyone else in your office miserable. You'll begin to dread having to talk to the person, regardless of how productive they may be. They'll bring down the morale of your whole office and degrade the culture. Maybe this has happened to you.

So, if shared values and cultural fit are so important, why don't more law offices consider these things when hiring? In an article from the Harvard Business Review online,[42:1] Alan Lewis, the owner of Grand Circle Travel, a $600 million international tour operator, explains how his company assesses the cultural fit of every hire. According to Lewis, hiring someone who doesn't fit with your values means you're hiring someone who is destined to fail.

> *I've found that in my business, alignment with my company's culture and values counts far more than do skills or experience. In most cases, if an associate shares our values, we can teach the job skills. That's why more than a decade ago we adopted a values-based hiring model. This decision has not only enhanced our recruiting efforts, it has contributed to the long-term success of our associates and of our organization.*
>
> *– ALAN LEWIS*

Here's the good news: You can build a high-performance team. Begin by first focusing on values and culture when hiring.

**1. Get very clear about what you expect from your people – both with respect to performance *and* values.** If you're not already crystal clear about your firm's culture and values, now's the time to get clear. You probably already know what you want in terms of competency from your people. That's the easy part. You know the level of competence you need in a paralegal or associate. Identifying the values you want your team to live by is much tougher. Being proactive, trustworthy, committed to excellent client service, and being a great team player are examples of values that you might expect from your people.

**Create a set of values for your firm.** Take time to identify and articulate your firm's values. Get input from everyone on the team. You can do this during a firm lunch. Here's a simple way to do it.

* Tell everyone that they are going to be part of creating the values for the firm. Explain that the firm's values will be the yardstick against which all behavior is measured – yours included.
* Give everyone a stack of sticky notes.
* Ask them to think of three values that they feel should be included in the values for the firm.
* Then write each value on a separate sticky note.
* Put the sticky notes on the wall. You'll likely see similar or even duplicate values identified. Group similar values together.
* Discuss each sticky note (or groups of notes). Let people explain why they chose a particular value.
* Ask questions:
  o Have we missed anything?
  o Do our values address the needs of our clients and how we deliver our services?
  o Do our values reflect how we want to treat each other?
  o Is there anything else we could/should add?
  o Is there anything we could/should change?
* After discussion, get everyone's agreement on the list of values for the firm by asking, "Is there anyone who doesn't feel that they can live by these values each day?"

Once everyone has agreed on the values for the firm, write them down, and make sure everyone has a copy at their desk. I recommend printing them and framing them. You can put a copy in your reception area and post them on your website, so that clients and potential clients can see them, too.

**2. When hiring, don't just ask candidates about their values; let them *show* you.** Observe candidates through all phases of the interview process. Are they polite and professional on the phone prior to their interview? Are they on time for their interview? Are they nice to your receptionist? How do they react if asked to take skill or behavioral assessments?

Use a two-step interview process, focusing on values first in the interview and skills in the second. Skills are the focus of the second interview because if you focus on skills first, you might eliminate someone who has the integrity, motivation, capacity, understanding and knowledge to be a perfect fit for your firm, but who may need training or experience in your practice area. And don't be afraid to put your candidates under some pressure during skills assessments. For example, ask a paralegal candidate to draft a simple motion for you as part of the interview process. How someone behaves under pressure is very revealing. Putting a bit of pressure on someone is like squeezing an orange. Why? Because as Dr. Wayne Dyer so eloquently once said, "When you squeeze an orange, orange juice comes out – because that's what's inside. When you are squeezed or put under pressure, what comes out is what's inside." I love that quote. When we are under pressure, we reveal ourselves. Pay attention when your candidates are under a bit of pressure during the interview process.

Once you are clear about your firm's values, hire and retain only those people who share them and will commit to living them. Period.

> *We've actually passed on a lot of really smart, talented*
> *people that we know can make an immediate impact on our*
> *top or bottom line, but if they're not good for the company*
> *culture, we won't hire them for that reason alone.*

> *– Tony Hsieh, Zappos CEO*

**3. Evaluate people not only with respect to their performance; measure how well they live the values of the firm.** Build your firm values into your evaluation process, then hold people accountable to them. Let everyone know that it's not enough to produce great work. Let them know that it's just as important for everyone to live by your firm's values. Everyone – including you.

**4. Get rid of anyone on your team whose values are inconsistent with your firm's values.** The hardest call to make is to let someone go who is a stellar performer, but who violates your firm's values. Someone who turns out the work and generates revenue for the firm, but is consistently late. Someone who is great with your clients, but rotten to other staff members. Someone who is "very experienced," but who creates a miserable experience for everyone else in the office. As difficult as it might be, you must remove those people from your team. The Jack Welch quote, below, from one of my favorite business books, *Up Your Business!*, says it all.

> *We made our leap forward when we began removing the people who hit the numbers but violated our values and making it clear to the entire company why they were asked to leave - not for the usual "personal reasons" or to "pursue other opportunities" but for not sharing our values. Until an organization develops the courage to do this, people never have full confidence that these values are real.*
> – From *Up Your Business! 7 Steps to Fix, Build, or Stretch Your Organization*[42:2]

If you're having personnel issues in your firm, there is a good chance that you have people on your team who can't or won't live the firm's values. Their values and those of your firm are in conflict. When this happens you need to address it immediately. For example, in the situation described above – a team member who is great at generating revenue, but who is always late – talk to that person first. Explain why his or her behavior is inconsistent with your firm's values (for example values of personal integrity and commitment) and that it must change. If it doesn't change, then you've got to let that person go. If you don't, then you'll lose the respect of everyone on your team.

And while you're at it, take a look in the mirror. Are you living up to the values you espouse? As the leader of your firm, you set the standard. You can't ask your people to live up to values that you don't live by...every single day.

## LIVING THE LESSON

* Write down the values that everyone in your firm will live by. Get input from everyone on your team when creating your values statement. Creating firm values, together with the firm's vision and mission, are great topics for a firm retreat.
* Make sure everyone on your team has a copy of the firm values on their desk.
* Don't allow the values to become merely nice words on paper. Use them as a measure in the hiring process. Build them into your evaluation process. Hold everyone on your team – that means you, too – accountable for living the values every day.
* Recognize team members who exemplify your values. Let go of those who don't.

[42:1] *"How My Company Hires for Culture First, Skills Second."* (2013). http:// blogs.hbr.org/2011/01/how-my-company-hires-for-cultu/ (Harvard Business Review HBR Blog Network).
[42:2] Anderson, Dave (2003). *Up Your Business! 7 Steps to Fix, Build, or Stretch Your Organization.* John Wiley & Sons, Inc.

## ADDITIONAL RESOURCES
*Hire Slow, Fire Fast: A Lawyer's Guide to Building a High Performance Team,* by Mark Powers and Shawn McNalis
*The Talent Advantage: How to Attract and Retain the Best and the Brightest,* by Alan Weiss and Nancy MacKay

*Lesson 43*

●  ●  ●  ●

# DOES YOUR TEAM ROCK? INSIST ON ONLY "A+" PLAYERS.

*I'm not interested in having an orchestra sound like
itself. I want it to sound like the composer.*

— *LEONARD BERNSTEIN*

Before I went to law school, I was a professional musician. I played the guitar
and sang. Still do – sometimes. Music has always been a really big part of my
life. In fact, my first TV memory was when the Beatles appeared on the Ed
Sullivan Show. I was only four years old, and I was glued to our black-and-
white TV. The next day, my dad bought me the "Meet the Beatles!" album.
I still have it.

I think of just about everything in terms of music. So when I think of a
law firm, I often think about it in terms of a band and all the "players" in the
band. If you're running your own law firm, you're both the composer and the
conductor. So how's your band? How do they sound? Do they sound like the
composer? Are they playing the songs on your playlist? And are they playing them the way you want them to sound? I hope you're thinking, "We are
totally awesome! We rock!" But if you're thinking, "Geez, we'd be laughed off
the stage," then it's time to do something about it.

## PROBLEM BANDMATES

I have good news and bad news for you. First, the bad news: If your band is not rocking along, ignoring that fact won't make it go away. Sticking your fingers in your ears and saying, "Nah, nah, nah – I can't hear you," didn't work when you were a kid. And its professional cousin, ignoring people problems in your office, doesn't work in the adult world. It just makes them worse. In fact, when you ignore a problem with someone in the band, it sends a message to everyone else that says, "I don't really care about you or your work environment, and I'm too busy, or too scared, to deal with this issue."

I talk with my clients a lot about the importance of working with "A" clients. Why? "A" clients are a pleasure to work with. They listen to your advice, they pay their bills, and they refer other "A" clients to you. The other great thing about "A" clients is that you love working with them. While there are some universal truths about "A" clients like the ones I've listed above, every attorney can add to the list with specific characteristics that are key for their "A" clients. One more thing: "A" clients also generate most of your firm's revenue. It is very important for you to know what constitutes an "A" client for your firm. (*See* Lesson 25. Stop taking "D" clients.)

Just as it's important for you to know what an "A" client (or matter) for your firm looks like, it's equally important for you to know what constitutes an "A" player on your team, or in your band. You need to let your team members know what you expect – clearly and unambiguously. (*See* Lesson 42. When hiring, experience matters. But not so much.) Let your team know what it takes to be – not just an "A" player, but an "A+" player. Write it down. Create an "A+ Player Agreement," and ask everyone to commit to being an "A+" player. Then, if someone starts to fall short of the mark, you can pull out the agreement and use it as a coaching tool to get them back on track.

People cannot excel if they don't know what's expected of them. Let your players know what you want from them. Be crystal clear about expectations. They will either play the right notes or they won't. But at least they'll know what music they are being asked to play.

*A small team of A+ players can run circles
around a giant team of B and C players.*

— *STEVE JOBS*

## INSIST ON ONLY "A+" PLAYERS.

If you're running your own law firm, you are the leader of the band. You get to pick your "band mates." You've got to surround yourself with "A+" players who support you and the vision, mission, and values of your firm. If you don't, you will not make beautiful music together. Here's how you can build a band that rocks.

**First:** Start paying attention to your players. Do you have the right people in your band? Are they all "A+" players? If not, why not? I can't stress how important this is. Think of Lawrence Welk backing up Mick Jagger. That's just wrong. Now think about Bruce Springsteen fronting the E Street Band. Perfect match.

**Second:** As the leader of your band, you get to write the songs and pick the playlist. You decide who plays a solo, and when. You even get to demand only green M&M's in your dressing room. You get the picture. You're the leader. You're The Boss . . . literally. So, be very clear about your expectations for each of your players.

**Third:** Practice, practice, practice. No matter how good the players, the band will never be awesome without lots and lots and lots of practice. So, meet with your band every day. Make sure everybody knows their part. Make sure the bass player is in step with the drummer and everybody is playing the same song at the same time.

This is where so many lawyers fall short. They simply don't take the time to practice and coach and mentor their people. Just like a great band or orchestra, in order to perform at your highest level, you've got to rehearse. There is no way around it.

Imagine yourself in this scenario: You buy tickets to see your favorite orchestra. You settle into your seat tingling with anticipation. The lights dim.

The musicians take their seats. The conductor walks on stage to thunderous applause, bows and says, "Well, we haven't rehearsed any of the pieces we're going to perform for you this evening. I hope everything goes okay." The scenario is absurd. And it is no less absurd to think that your office can function at its best by just winging it.

> If you don't invest time and money in good people, you don't deserve them. In fact, you deserve to lose them, and probably will. It's just a matter of time.
>     – From *Up Your Business! 7 Steps to Fix, Build, or Stretch Your Organization*

It's up to you to set the stage for success. Insist on "A+" players. Let them know exactly what is expected of them. Do your part by practicing, coaching, and mentoring. Then give your band a "shout out," and raise your lighter in the air (or your mobile phone, depending upon your generation) because you're on your way to stardom. Of course, like in any great band, the practicing never stops. But taking these first three steps will get you moving in the right direction.

Rock on.

## LIVING THE LESSON

* Do you have the right people in your band? If not, you need to either replace them with the right people, or make sure that you are giving them the resources, support, and encouragement they need to become "A+" players.
* Set clear expectations for everyone in your office. Let each person know exactly what it takes to be an "A+" player.

\* Practice, practice, practice. At the very least, schedule weekly meetings with your key players.
  o Review deadlines.
  o Set goals and priorities for the coming week.
  o Adjust as needed.

## ADDITIONAL RESOURCES

*Up Your Business! 7 Steps to Fix, Build, or Stretch Your Organization*, by Dave Anderson

# *Lesson 44*

● ● ● ●

## MONEY MATTERS, BUT IT'S NOT THE MOST IMPORTANT THING.

*People are entitled to joy in work.*

— W. EDWARDS DEMING

Leaders at many law firms give little thought to how their firms' compensation plans are structured. And while everyone wants to be paid well for their work, in terms of compensation, the old saying is true: Money isn't everything. And it definitely isn't the only thing. I'm not saying that monetary compensation isn't important. It is. What I'm saying is that if you're focused solely on dollars, you're not likely to attract *and* retain the best and the brightest.

In his book, *Drive: The Surprising Truth About What Motivates Us*,[44:1] Daniel Pink explains that money can actually be demotivating. This concept has proven true time after time based on years of behavioral and motivational research.

When organizations use rewards like money to motivate staff, that's when they're most demotivating. The better strategy is to get compensation right – and then get it out of sight. Effective organizations compensate people in amounts and ways that allow individuals to mostly forget about compensation and instead focus on the work itself.

- From *Drive: The Surprising Truth About What Motivates Us*

While this may sound counterintuitive, think about it for a moment. Pink isn't suggesting that you underpay your people. Rather, he suggests that you pay *more* than average. Paying your people at or above what the market is paying is important to both attracting and retaining great people. Yet competitive pay is just one part of the compensation equation. Pink's thinking isn't new. It is grounded in the work of W. Edwards Deming, a statistician and management consultant, who helped turn around the Japanese car industry after World War II. Dr. Deming is one of the founding fathers of the quality movement. He wrote extensively on the importance of recognizing workers beyond merely providing a paycheck. In fact, Dr. Deming's research also demonstrated that, beyond a certain point, monetary rewards can actually be demotivating.

What [our present style of reward systems] do is to squeeze out from an individual, over his lifetime, his innate intrinsic motivation, self-esteem, dignity. They build into him fear, self-defense, extrinsic motivation. We have been destroying our people, from toddlers on through the university, and on the job. We must preserve the power of intrinsic motivation, dignity, cooperation, curiosity, joy in learning, that people are born with.

-From *The New Economics for Industry, Government, Education*[44:2]

In fact, database research maintained by the Saratoga Institute of 19,700 exit interviews and current employee surveys conducted from 1999 through 2003, found that compensation issues represented only 12 percent of all reasons employees leave their jobs. In *The 7 Hidden Reasons Employees Leave: How to Recognize the Subtle Signs and Act Before It's Too Late,*[44:3] Leigh Branham reports the findings of the Saratoga Institute which make clear that money alone will not keep your best people from leaving you.

So when you think about compensation for your staff and associates, you've got to think about more than just dollars. Here are just a few of the hidden reasons, other than pay, why employees leave, according to Burnham:

* The workplace was not as expected: Sometimes, information provided during the hiring process, such as the type of work that will be assigned, how often employees are expected to work late, the possibility of advancement, and other matters don't turn out as "promised." Everyone is on their best behavior during the hiring process – candidates *and* you and your team. Have you ever painted a rosier than reality picture of your office to potential candidates?

* Too little coaching and feedback: When was the last time you spent an hour each month with your key people – staff or associates – just to coach and develop them? One hour a month is less than one percent of the typical 160 hours an employee works in a month.

* Feeling devalued and unrecognized: How often do you say "thank you?" or truly acknowledge a job well-done?

* Stress from overwork and lack of work-life balance: Does your firm offer flex time? Are your people stressed out because you're addicted to the adrenaline rush of working on a deadline?

* Loss of trust and confidence in leadership: Are you really leading your firm? Or are you so caught up in the work that you don't really have time for your people?

If you still think retention is mainly about money, find out how much it is costing your competition to get people to leave you. That's called your "poach rate." If your poach rate is less than 20 percent, it ain't the money, honey! People who love their work, love their boss, and love their company don't leave unless the offer is coming from the Godfather.

— From *The 7 Hidden Reasons Employees Leave: How to Recognize the Subtle Signs and Act Before It's Too Late*

Even in the years since 2009 – during the deepest recession in decades – studies continue to show that money alone is not sufficient compensation to keep people engaged in the work they do. Employees who are engaged are happy, productive, successful, care about clients, and typically stay in their jobs. Engaged employees are passionate about the work they do and feel a deep connection to the company they work for. While the idea of engagement may sound all warm and fuzzy to attorneys, it's clear that engaged employees can make a huge impact on the firm's bottom line. In fact, a study published by Gallup in 2013 found that businesses with high levels of employee engagement experienced 147% higher earnings per share for stockholders than their competitors. On the flip side, Gallup estimates that active disengagement costs the U.S. economy $450 to $450 billion per year.[44:4]

If you could increase client satisfaction AND reduce employee turnover AND benefit your bottom line by creating more engaged employees, why not give it a shot? The good news is that creating engaged employees will cost you nothing more than time, attention, and your sincere desire to start acknowledging members of your team when they are doing something right. (*See* Lesson 46. Say "thank you" every day, and mean it.)

> Yes, compensation and incentives are important, but for very different reasons in good-to-great companies. The purpose of a compensation system should not be to get the right behaviors from the wrong people, but to get the right people on the bus in the first place, and to keep them there.
> - From *Good to Great: Why Some Companies Make the Leap...And Others Don't*[44:5]

So start thinking beyond just money when you think of compensation. Compensation includes the sum and substance of what it means to work at your firm. When you evaluate your compensation systems, be sure to include non-monetary compensation, and don't leave your firm vulnerable to the poachers.

Money without meaning is not enough compensation.
– From *12: The Elements of Great Managing*[44:6]

## LIVING THE LESSON

* Before evaluating your compensation and the level of engagement of your people, make sure you have the right people on your team. (*See* Lesson 43. Does your team rock? Insist on only "A+" players.)
* Focus on people's strengths – not their weaknesses. Allow your people to play to their strengths by making sure you have the right people in the right positions. According to the Gallup research, people who use their strengths every day are six times more likely to be engaged at work.
* Rather than thinking solely in terms of monetary rewards, ask yourself and your team what you and the firm can do to enhance their overall well-being. Too many law firms merely give lip service to the importance of work-life balance. They give little consideration to the concept in reality. Don't be one of those law firms.

[44:1] Pink, Daniel H. (2011). *Drive: The Surprising Truth About What Motivates Us*. Riverhead Books.

[44:2] Deming, W. Edwards (2nd Edition 2000). *The New Economics for Industry, Government, Education*. The MIT Press.

[44:3] Branham, Leigh (2004). *The 7 Hidden Reasons Employees Leave: How to Recognize the Subtle Signs and Act Before It's Too Late*. AMACOM.

[44:4] State of the American Workplace 2013, published by Gallup. You can download a copy of the report here: http://www.gallup.com/strategic consulting/163007/state-american-workplace.aspx

[44:5] Collins, Jim (2001). *Good to Great: Why Some Companies Make the Leap...And Others Don't*. HarperBusiness.

[44:6] Harter, James K., and Wagner, Rodd (2006). 1*2: The Elements of Great Managing*. Gallup Press.

## ADDITIONAL RESOURCES

*First, Break All the Rules: What the World's Greatest Managers Do Differently*, by Marcus Buckingham and Curt Coffman.

*The Talent Advantage: How to Attract and Retain the Best and the Brightest*, by Alan Weiss and Nancy MacKay.

## *Lesson 45*

●  ●  ●  ●

# CHECK IN ON PEOPLE. DON'T CHECK UP ON THEM.

*The people we develop execute and carry the torch for the
things we care about—and then take the organization up,
up and far beyond what we or they had imagined possible.*

— TOM PETERS

When was the last time you asked someone who works with you, "How are
you doing?" and then really listened to the answer? Not, "What are you
working on?" Not, "Did you finish that draft memo?" But "How are YOU
doing?" It seems like such a simple question. It is a simple question. Yet those
four words, when asked sincerely, are quite powerful. They say you care about
the person, not just the work being done. That's important because when
people feel like their employer really cares about them, they're much more
likely to be engaged in their work. Love their work. Do better work. Treat
clients better. And treat each other better. (*See* Lesson 46. Say "thank you"
every day, and mean it.)

All too often, lawyers are so entrenched in the work being done that they
see the people they work with as merely the means to an end. They are there
to get the work done. You may have hired your team to get the work done, but

that's not WHY they work for you. (*See* Lesson 44. Money matters, but it's not the most important thing.) If you're lucky, your people work for you because they love the work and have the opportunity to bring their best selves to work every day. If your people are bringing their best selves to work every day, then they are going to do great work. And YOU can have a big impact on whether your team is bringing their best selves to work every day. YOU can influence how engaged your team is and whether they are doing their best work. You can do this by starting with a simple question, "How are you doing?"

Sound too touchy-feely and mushy for you? Think again. Checking in on people, instead of checking up on them, costs you nothing but a few moments of your time, and the payoff can be monumental.

## PRACTICE MANAGEMENT BY WANDERING AROUND AND "GOING TO THE GEMBA"

Tom Peters is known for popularizing the phrase "management by wandering around (MBWA)." He learned it from Bill Hewlett and Dave Packard while working as a consultant with McKinsey & Co. When Peters wrote about MBWA in *In Search of Excellence*[45:1] in 1982, the idea was new to most managers. Although MBWA quickly caught on as a powerful way to create an engaged workforce, it doesn't come naturally to everyone. If it doesn't come naturally to you, consider giving it a try. It can help you build an engaged team, improve productivity, and may even give you a fresh perspective on how effectively your firm operates.

> So, management by wandering around is the business of staying in touch with the territory all the time. It has the extra benefit of getting you off your chair and moving around your area. By wandering around I literally mean moving around and talking to people. It's all done on a very informal and spontaneous basis, but it's important in the course of time to cover the whole territory. You start out by being accessible and approachable, but the main thing is to realize you're there to listen. The second is that it is vital to keep people informed about what's going on in the company, especially those things that

are important to them. The third reason for doing this is because it is just plain fun.
   – From *In Search of Excellence*

Although *In Search of Excellence* may have made MBWA a part of the management lexicon, the concept of MBWA has been around for a long time. In fact, some historians claim that Abraham Lincoln was one of its first practitioners because of his habit of informally reviewing and talking with his troops during the Civil War. More recently, MBWA was (and is) an integral part of the Total Quality Management movement (TQM) and Lean. Lean is a process for continuous improvement adopted with great success by the Japanese automotive industry after WWII. "Going to the gemba," a key management practice in Lean, is a Japanese phrase that means to "go and see" where the work is being done. Although your law firm is not an automobile factory, there is much be achieved by "going to the gemba."

MBWA and going to the gemba give you an opportunity to check in on people, not check up on them. In *The Outstanding Organization*,[45:2] author Karen Martin explains two specific purposes for the practice. The first is to gain better clarity about how work is being done. Do your people have what they need to do their work effectively and efficiently? Are there bottlenecks in the process that you don't even know about? The second purpose is to gain insights from the people actually doing the work. The people on your team have much more knowledge than you may give them credit for. They may have great ideas on how to improve workflow processes. Ask them.

The clarity that is achieved by "going and seeing" trumps information discussed in offices, meetings rooms, and hallways, which leads to far better decisions, more robust problem solving, and an increased level of understanding that builds outstanding organizations.
   – From *The Outstanding Organization: Generate Business Results by Eliminating Chaos and Building the Foundation for Everyday Excellence*

At first, people may wonder what in the world you're doing coming out of your office to ask how they are. They might think you're interfering or trying to spy on them or maybe even think you've just lost your mind. But the suspicion will quickly fade and be replaced with engaged employees once everyone begins to see the benefits of checking in, not checking up.

## LIVING THE LESSON

* Make MBWA a habit, part of your daily routine, but not at a fixed time.
* Be sure to visit everyone on the team. Don't leave people out.
* Ask the question: "How are you doing?" You can follow up with questions like: "Do you have everything you need?" "Is there anything you need from me?"
* Be sure to honor your team's focus time. (*See* Lesson 9. Learn to manage needless interruptions or you'll never be able to focus on anything). Don't interrupt them during their focus time.
* Ask for suggestions and ideas. Don't use this time to critique.
* Listen. (*See* Lesson 35. Learn how to listen. Really listen).

[45:1] Waterman, Robert, and Peters, Tom (2006). *In Search of Excellence: Lessons From America's Best-Run Companies.* HarperBusiness.
[45:2] Martin, Karen (2012). *The Outstanding Organization; Generate Business Results by Eliminating Chaos and Building the Foundation for Everyday Excellence.* McGraw-Hill.

## ADDITIONAL RESOURCES

*The Every Day MBA Series: Management by Walking Around,* by Colin Barrow.
*The Circle of Innovation,* by Tom Peters.

*Lesson 46*

● ● ● ●

# SAY "THANK YOU" EVERY DAY, AND MEAN IT.

*The deepest principle in human nature
is the craving to be appreciated.*

— WILLIAM JAMES

## WHY APPRECIATION IS SO IMPORTANT

Developing and retaining great people is not as simple as saying "thank you." And it's not as simple as saying "I'm sorry." (*See* Lesson 37. Say "I'm sorry" when you make a mistake.) But these two phrases, when said with sincerity, demonstrate a sense of genuine caring for other people. And a workplace culture that is supportive and caring is a culture that will help to create engaged employees. "So what?" you may be thinking. "What the heck is an engaged employee, and, more importantly, why should I care?" Engaged employees are essential to the health and growth of your firm. Engaged employees are happier, more productive, and more client-focused. That translates into more profit for your firm and a much more resonant environment – a place that people look forward to coming to each morning, rather than dreading. (For more on the importance of cultivating a resonant environment, *see* Lesson 41. Check your attitude at the door.)

Engaged employees impact your productivity and profitability line in a very positive way. Disengaged employees not only diminish productivity and profitability, they'll drag other employees down, destroy morale, and drive away clients.

In the book, *How Full is Your Bucket?*,[46:1] authors Tom Rath and Donald O. Clifton cite a U.S. Department of Labor Study which found that the number-one reason people leave their jobs is that they don't feel appreciated on a day-to-day basis. In other words, they are not engaged. But people who do feel appreciated are more likely to be engaged. An engaged employee shows up on time (or early), stays late when needed, smiles, shows enthusiasm, is a great team player, is an ambassador for the firm, and truly cares about the firm and its mission. And a great side benefit of having engaged employees is that they recruit other engaged employees!

On the other hand, people who don't feel appreciated are more likely to be disengaged from work. A disengaged employee will not only make your life miserable, he'll make the lives of everyone around him miserable, *and* he'll tell others that your firm is a horrible place to work. You do not want disengaged people in your office.

Your mission – should you choose to accept it – is to create a firm culture that develops and supports engaged employees. Here are some characteristics that most engaged employees share:

* They use their talents and strengths every day.
* They are consistently high performers.
* They are team players who build supportive relationships.
* They have high levels of energy and enthusiasm.
* They focus on getting their work done in a proactive way.
* They are emotionally committed to what they do.
* They are committed to the firm and the clients you serve.

Imagine for just a moment what it would feel like to walk into your office each morning and be greeted by a team of engaged employees. Yes, I can see you smiling. But having a team of engaged employees will do much more than just make you feel great and help you serve your clients better. It will make your firm more profitable.

## ENGAGED EMPLOYEES CREATE ENGAGED CUSTOMERS

In the book *Follow This Path: How the World's Greatest Organizations Unleash Human Potential*,[46:2] authors Curt Coffman and Gabriel Gonzalez-Molina analyzed research from the Gallup Organization's study of more than 10 million customers, three million employees, and 200,000 managers. According to the authors, engaged employees "are involved in generating *all* of an organization's profits and customer engagement." Customer engagement goes far beyond merely customer loyalty or satisfaction. Engaged customers are "A+" clients. They literally add value to your business by speaking well of you and your firm and referring other "A+" clients to you. They will return to you for legal work. Quite simply, they will generate more profit for your firm.

Here's the bottom line: Engaged employees will improve your bottom line – significantly. Hundreds of Gallup studies have demonstrated time and time again the positive impact engaged employees have on a business. Businesses with employee engagement scores in the top half as compared to those in the bottom half have, on average:

* 86 percent higher customer satisfaction ratings
* 70 percent more success in lowering turnover
* 70 percent higher productivity
* 44 percent higher profitability

Did you get that last one? *Forty-four percent higher profitability*. Engaged employees are positive, happy people who work hard and treat your clients well. And they have the capacity to improve your bottom line by 44 percent. But even if engaged employees only improved your bottom line by 10 percent or 15 percent, wouldn't it be worth having a team of these awesome people around you?

> Enterprises that wouldn't think of letting an accounting school dropout run its finances, a Luddite run IT, or a klutz supervise safety, routinely let dislikable, insincere, or aloof men and women assume stewardship for a crew of the company's ostensibly greatest assets.
> - From *12: The Elements of Great Managing*[46:3]

## CREATING ENGAGEMENT: SHOW YOUR APPRECIATION AND GET SPECIFIC

So what can you do to help ensure that your employees are engaged and not disengaged? Begin by creating a culture that supports engagement and recruit and hire employees who will fit your culture. Then, make it a habit to show your genuine appreciation for the work they do. Not just one or two days a year, but every day. Giving sincere recognition is one of the most powerful things you can do to create engagement. Say "thank you" even for the little things. It's okay – really – and it doesn't cost you anything. Caveat: The key here is "sincere recognition." People know when they're being manipulated. If you're saying thank you while at the same time perpetuating a miserable culture, you're going to have problems.

Have you ever noticed that when you're giving someone constructive criticism, you're very specific? Yet, when you praise someone it's likely a very general, "nice job!" Guess what? Our brains remember the specific, not the general. That's why we often can remember a piece of stinging criticism for years, but have trouble remembering a time when we felt truly appreciated. So work hard to get specific with your praise. Be aware of how often you correct or criticize someone on your team, and make a conscious effort to look for ways to acknowledge them when you can. If you show your appreciation daily, and get specific with your praise, your employees will show their appreciation by showing up engaged. It won't cost you a penny. And remember, all the money in the world can't buy an engaged employee. Your firm's culture either creates an atmosphere that allows engaged employees to flourish, or it creates an atmosphere that feeds disengaged employees. It's all up to you. (*See* Lesson 44. Money matters, but it's not the most important thing.)

## LIVING THE LESSON

* Make it a habit to look for ways to consistently acknowledge the people on your team. Make it genuine!
* Start your day by sending a one-sentence email thanking or acknowledging a team member for work they've done. The more specific you

are, the more meaningful and memorable your words will be. *Caveat: Do this only if you are sincere. Don't force it or be phony.*

\* Ask everyone on your team whether they feel they receive the support and professional development they need to be their best. Listen to their feedback and provide them with additional resources, if necessary.

[46:1] Clifton, Donald O. and Rath, Tom (2004). *How Full is Your Bucket?* Gallup Press.

[46:2] Gonzalez-Molina, Gabriel, and Coffman, Curt (2002). *Follow This Path: How the World's Greatest Organizations Unleash Human Potential.* Business Plus.

[46:3] Harter, James K., and Wagner, Rodd (2006). *12: The Elements of Great Managing.* Gallup Press.

*Lesson 47*

● ● ● ●

## GIVE VOICE TO LEADERSHIP.

*The key to successful leadership today is influence, not authority.*

— KEN BLANCHARD

Leadership. Millions of words have been written about that one word. Yet understanding leadership doesn't have to be difficult or complicated. Leadership is not – as the old saying goes – rocket science. Leadership is human science. Leadership is not about position or titles. It is not about authority or power. The essence of leadership is about understanding yourself and others. Leadership is about influencing others. And while leadership may be difficult to define, to paraphrase Justice Potter Stewart in *Jacobellis v. Ohio,* "You know it when you see it."

Leadership can exist at any level in an organization. In the best organizations, leadership does exist at every level. Regardless of whether you are a sole practitioner, managing partner, paralegal or law clerk, you are a leader. And you should strive to build leadership at every level in your firm.

*Every organization must have not one but many
leaders. Leadership is a responsibility shared
by all members of the organization.*

— FRANCES HESSELBEIN

So, millions of words have been written about a concept that is difficult to define; yet we know it when we see it. Is it possible to distill all that leadership is into a concept that can be drawn upon and put into action every day? In an effort to add only slightly to the lexicon of leadership, I offer the acronym VOICE. You can give VOICE to leadership each day in all that you do. Let's take a look at the components of VOICE.

## V: VISION – LEADERS CREATE A VISION THAT PULLS THEM FORWARD IN A POSITIVE WAY.

Lawyers are leaders. No other profession has given us more leaders in our communities, our country or our world. And leaders know that leadership is about vision. Leaders don't dwell on problems and bemoan what is wrong. Instead, they focus on possibility. They envision what could be. They are inspired by the vision of a positive future, and they are inspiring to those around them. Great leaders don't focus on what's wrong; they focus on solutions. And then they work to inspire others to help them make their vision a reality. Leaders create a vision that pulls them forward in a positive way. Here are three elements to consider when creating your vision:

* Authentic. Your vision should be authentic. Be true to yourself and your values.
* Aligned. Your vision should be aligned with your personal and professional goals.
* Inspiring. Your vision should inspire and excite you. It is the magnet that pulls you toward a great future.

The goal is not to speculate about what might happen, but to imagine what you can make happen.

– From *Leading the Revolution, by Gary Hamel*

## 0: "OWN IT" – KNOW YOUR STRENGTHS AND WEAKNESSES. LEADERS ARE SELF-AWARE.

Self-awareness means understanding ourselves – and understanding how we are perceived by others.

Why is self-awareness important? Because without self-awareness, we can get caught up in behaviors that are inconsistent with our own values and beliefs. Without self-awareness, we may not have the courage to say "no" to the unimportant things in life so that we can focus on the truly important.

Without self-awareness, leaders may fear appearing vulnerable. Without self-awareness, leaders can't understand how their characteristics and behaviors impact other people. Self-awareness is the ability to understand ourselves and our characteristics, and utilize our characteristics in ways that serve us best. (*See* Lesson 40. Get to know yourself.)

Self-awareness is the foundation for growth and positive change, but it doesn't just happen. You've got to work at it. Here are a few suggestions to get you started.

* Cultivate self-awareness. You can begin the process by taking a self-assessment such as DISC. DISC measures your preferred behaviors. DISC gives you valuable insights to your own behaviors. It gives you the ability to see yourself as others see you and understand the impact your behaviors have on those around you.
* Ask for feedback. Regardless of whether you take a DISC assessment or other type of self-assessment, ask for feedback from those around you. For example, if you want to become a better listener, let people know you're working on your listening skills and ask for feedback on how you're doing.
* Commit to continuously improving. Self-awareness is a never-ending process. Always be striving to be better than you are today.

*Knowing yourself is the beginning of all wisdom.*

*— ARISTOTLE*

## I: INFLUENCE – LEADERS KNOW HOW TO INFLUENCE OTHERS AND MOLD CONSENSUS.

The days of "my way or the highway" leadership are over. There was a time when leadership was thought of as mere strength. In today's world, an autocratic, dictatorial leadership style just doesn't work. Even worse, it's damaging. It leads to one-way communication and misunderstandings. Regardless of whether you're leading the people in your office, an executive board, or your family, understanding and appreciating people's differences will help you influence them to your point of view.

* No more MWOTH. "My way or the highway" isn't leadership, it's dictatorship. And no one wants to work for a dictator.
* Think: Collaboration. Always be open to ideas and suggestions from those around you.
* Appreciate people's differences. Show respect for everyone you work with.

*Leadership is not about titles, positions or flowcharts.*
*It is about one life influencing another.*

*— JOHN C. MAXWELL*

## C: COMMUNICATION – LEADERS KNOW HOW TO COMMUNICATE EFFECTIVELY.

Communication is one of the most important skills in life. And while at least half of the communication equation involves listening, most of us have little or no training in listening – really listening. In fact, various listening studies have shown that we remember between 25% and 50% of what we hear. So the best way to improve your communication is to practice being a better listener.

Here are three things that I promise will improve your communication:

* Be present. Don't interrupt or finish the other person's sentences. And don't be distracted – focus on the person you're speaking with.
* Listen. (*See* Lesson 35. Learn how to listen. Really listen.)
* Seek to understand. At our core as human beings, we want to be understood. Honor the people you interact with by seeking to understand their interests in any situation.

*The way we communicate with others and with ourselves*
*ultimately determines the quality of our lives.*

— ANTHONY ROBBINS

## E: EXAMPLE – LEADERS WALK THE TALK AND LEAD BY EXAMPLE.

Do you bring a positive attitude to the office every day? Remember that as a leader, everything you do matters. Everything. Look at the culture of your office. Is it positive or negative? Whatever the culture, it is a reflection of the leadership. It is a reflection of your attitude. If you're in a good mood, chances are others will be, too. If you're in a bad mood, they'll pick up on that too. Here's the good news: You can make a conscious decision to change your attitude at any time. As a leader, it's your job to model the kinds of attitudes and behaviors you want to encourage in your team. You set the tone for your office. So, make a conscious choice to set a good tone. (*See* Lesson 41. Check your attitude at the door.)

Remember:

* Everything matters. Everything.
* Smile. Genuinely smile. In *Enchantment: The Art of Changing Hearts, Minds, and Actions*,[47:1] Guy Kawasaki encourages us to "make crow's feet" when we smile. A genuine smile involves your whole face – especially your eyes.

* Fake it. If you can't smile genuinely, fake it. Fake it. As Harvard Professor Amy Cuddy says, "Fake it until you become it."

> *Example is not the main thing in influencing others. It is the only thing.*
>
> — ALBERT SCHWEITZER

Leadership may not be rocket science; but if you remember these five components of leadership and act on them, you can give VOICE to leadership every day.

## LIVING THE LESSON

* Look for ways each day to:
  o Share your vision
  o Develop your self-awareness
  o Influence and inspire others
  o Improve your communication skills
  o Set an example for those around you

[47:1] Kawasaki, Guy (2011). *Enchantment: The Art of Changing Hearts, Minds, and Actions.* Penguin Group.

## ADDITIONAL RESOURCES

*Presence: Bringing Your Boldest Self to Your Biggest Challenges,* by Amy Cuddy.
*What Got You Here, Won't Get You There,* by Marshall Goldsmith.
*Leading the Revolution,* by Gary Hamel.
*Confidence,* by Rosabeth Moss Kanter.

*Lesson 48*

● ● ● ●

# TRUST YOUR GUT.

*I believe in intuitions and inspirations...I sometimes
feel that I am right. I do not know that I am.*

— *ALBERT EINSTEIN*

## HOW DO YOU MAKE DECISIONS?

As a lawyer, you're called upon to make dozens of decisions each day. You're making decisions regarding administrative issues in your office. You're making decisions about how to proceed in a particular piece of litigation. You're deciding whether to take on that new client who really wants to work with you and is ready to write you a big check, but something just doesn't feel right.

Have you ever thought about HOW you make decisions? I'm guessing your first thought is something like, "Well, I investigate, review all the facts, and then I make a rational, objective decision based on the facts." Most lawyers I know feel pretty strongly that emotions shouldn't have any place in decision making. But the truth is, emotions or gut feelings help us make decisions. And listening to our gut will often help us make *better* decisions.

## WHY GUT FEELINGS ARE IMPORTANT, AND WHY YOU SHOULD LISTEN TO THEM.

Antonio Damasio, director of the Brain and Creativity Institute at the University of Southern California and author of *Descartes' Error: Emotion, Reason, and the Human Brain*,[48:1] has written several books on how our emotions are critical to our decision-making process. Damasio refers to intuition and "gut feelings" as somatic markers. Somatic markers, according to Damasio, "mark" certain situations with emotion. We are collecting somatic markers throughout our lives. When we experience something – good or bad – we don't just remember the facts of the situation. We remember how the situation made us feel. We remember our emotions in the context of the situation. But we can't call up our somatic markers from our conscious brain as explicit memories. Instead, these markers are stored in our subconscious, as implicit memories, which arise as gut feelings. According to Damasio, when somatic markers are present *and* we pay attention to them, we make better decisions.

> In short, somatic markers are a special instance of feelings generated from secondary emotions. Those emotions and feelings have been connected, by learning, to predicted future outcomes of certain scenarios. When a negative somatic marker is juxtaposed to a particular future outcome the combination functions as an alarm bell. When a positive somatic marker is juxtaposed instead, it becomes a beacon of incentive.
>
> - From *Descartes' Error: Emotion, Reason, and the Human Brain*

Somatic markers are the reason why (I hope) you won't take on that potential client I described above. When something just doesn't feel right, and you can't articulate why, that's a somatic marker talking. "It's just a feeling," you say. And you are exactly correct. What would happen if you ignored that feeling? You know the answer, because you've lived it. You take on that client who really wants to work with you, who's ready to write a big check, but you have this nagging feeling that something's not right. And that client turns into the client from hell. You knew this would happen. Your gut told you so.

Listening to your gut is also crucial to developing your emotional intelligence. While your legal skill and substantive knowledge is grounded in fact, your ability to relate to your clients, persuade a jury, or negotiate with opposing counsel is grounded in emotion. And our emotions simply don't speak the same language as facts. We need to listen to those gut feelings because they are the only way our emotions – our wisdom – can get through to our brains. Our brains can't express our somatic markers in words.

> [I]nstead, the emotional brain activates circuitry that runs from the limbic centers into the gut, giving us the compelling sense that this feels right [or wrong]. The amygdala, then, lets us know its conclusions primarily through circuitry extending into the gastrointestinal tract that, literally, creates a gut feeling. Gut feelings offer a guide when facing a complex decision that goes beyond the data at hand. Gut feeling, in fact, has gained new scientific respect because of recent discoveries about implicit learning— that is, the lessons in life we pick up without being aware that we're learning them.
> - From *Primal Leadership: Unleashing the Power of Emotional Intelligence*[48:2]

Now, don't get me wrong. I'm not saying that facts don't matter. They do. Both facts and emotion are essential to good decision making. The challenge for fact-focused lawyers is to appreciate the importance of emotion in the mix. What we call wisdom is not built upon facts. Rather, wisdom is what we learn from our emotions.

Emotions are not impediments to good decision making – they are essential to it.


## LIVING THE LESSON

*   Pay attention to how you are making decisions. Do you listen to your gut?

* Try this experiment: Keep a "journal" of your gut feelings and subsequent decisions. You can keep a written journal or dictate notes into your phone. Do this for a month and track:
  o A brief description of the situation, relevant facts, and your "gut feeling."
  o The decision you made.
  o Whether your gut was right.

[48:1] Damasio, Antonio (2005). *Descartes' Error: Emotion, Reason, and the Human Brain*. Penguin Books.

[48:2] Goleman, Daniel, Boyatzis, Richard, and McKee, Annie (2002). *Primal Leadership: Unleashing the Power of Emotional Intelligence*. Harvard Business Review Press.

*Lesson 49*

●　　●　　●　　●

## CULTIVATE POSITIVITY. GIVE THANKS. GIVE BACK.

*Positivity doesn't just change the contents of your
mind, trading bad thoughts for good ones; it also
changes the scope or boundaries of your mind. It
widens the span of possibilities that you see.*

— BARBARA FREDRICKSON

Do you know the expression "attitude of gratitude"? The idea of being grateful
for the good things in life is a simple one. Regardless of what's going on in
our lives, there is always something to be grateful for, although sometimes the
stress of life makes it difficult to see those things. But there's a very good reason to look closely for those things in life that we can be grateful for. Feelings
of gratitude cultivate positivity in your brain. Positivity is good for your brain
because it helps you to think more clearly and creatively. Here's why.

### WHY POSITIVITY MATTERS

In her book, *Positivity: Groundbreaking Research Reveals How to Embrace the
Hidden Strength of Positive Emotions, Overcome Negativity, and Thrive,*[49:1]

Barbara Fredrickson, one of the leading researchers on the effect of positive emotions on brain function, explains that cultivating the emotion of gratitude is a powerful way to bring more positivity into your life. Positivity is important because our brains work better when we are feeling positive.

> The latest scientific evidence tells us that positivity doesn't simply reflect success and health, it can also produce success and health. This means that even after positivity fades, we can find traces of its impact. Beyond the present pleasant moment, your positivity has downstream consequences for the very trajectory of your life. Positivity spells the difference between whether you languish or flourish.
> - From *Positivity: Groundbreaking Research Reveals How to Embrace the Hidden Strength of Positive Emotions, Overcome Negativity, and Thrive*

Research has demonstrated that exercise can create what's known as a "runner's high." Runner's high is a feeling of euphoria created by the release of potent chemicals in the body. Research has also shown that feeling positive emotions can lead to the same good feelings. And feeling good not only feels good, it helps our brains function more effectively.

> Positive emotions flood our brains with dopamine and serotonin, chemicals that not only make us feel good, but dial up the learning centers of our brains to higher levels. They help us organize new information, keep that information in the brain longer, and retrieve it faster later on. And they enable us to make and sustain more neural connections, which allows us to think more quickly and creatively, become more skilled at complex analysis and problem solving, and see and invent new ways of doing things.
> - From *The Happiness Advantage: The Seven Principles of Positive Psychology That Fuel Success and Performance at Work*[49:2]

When we are in a positive state of mind, our peripheral vision improves. We actually see more of the world around us. We can take in and process information more effectively. The ability to see more – literally – allows us to also see more – figuratively. What I mean is that when we are in a positive state of mind, we can see unique solutions to problems that we might not even notice if we are in a negative state. Think of your work as a lawyer. How often do you feel positive emotions during a typical workday? The paradox is that the work lawyers do can lead to an overdose of negative emotions when the exact opposite is what your brain needs in order to be at its creative best.

## POSITIVITY AND GRATITUDE – A POWERFUL COMBINATION.

So if being positive can actually help our brains function more effectively, how do we get more of it into our lives? One way is to be grateful for the good things in life. Gratitude is one of the best ways to cultivate more positivity. Dr. Robert Emmons, a pioneer in gratitude research at the University of California, Davis, has shown that maintaining an attitude of gratitude is not only good for you, it can improve your overall health, including your psychological, emotional, and physical well-being. Being grateful forces people to overcome what psychologists call the "negativity bias." The negativity bias is our tendency to dwell on problems and annoyances rather than happy or uplifting events. Moreover, focusing on what's good in your life can also help you ward off depression and deal more effectively with stress.

## ACTIVATE FEELINGS OF GRATITUDE AND POSITIVITY BY GIVING BACK.

When we're motivated by a true spirit of generosity, we benefit as much as those on the receiving end. Jesuit priest Anthony de Mello says it this way: "Charity is really self-interest masquerading under the form of altruism. ...I give myself the pleasure of pleasing others." In the same vein, the Dalai Lama playfully speaks of working to benefit others as "selfish altruism." According to the Social Capital Community Benchmark Survey,[49:3] overseen by researchers from Harvard University, those who gave contributions of time or money were "42 percent more likely to be happy" than those who didn't give.

Just as exercise can create a runner's high, giving back creates what psychologists call a "helper's high." A "helper's high" is a state of euphoria created by a release of endorphins in the brain – just like a runner's high. In his book, *365 Thank Yous: The Year a Simple Act of Daily Gratitude Changed my Life,*[49:4] attorney John Kralik tells of how his commitment to writing a thank-you note every day for a year truly changed his life.

Kralik focused on the art of the thank-you note to cultivate his attitude of gratitude. What can you do? Begin now to create your "attitude of gratitude." Why not start by writing a thank-you note to each of your best referral sources? Keep them simple and sincere. Chances are you'll feel great after writing them. And that's something to be grateful for.

## LIVING THE LESSON

* Cultivate positivity by increasing your daily gratitude factor. Keep a gratitude journal. You can do this in a paper journal or on your phone or tablet. Each night before you go to sleep, write down three things that you are grateful for. This exercise asks you to look back on your day and notice the good things in your life. Also, it helps you to begin noticing things to be grateful for during the day.
* Cultivate positivity by giving back. Think of ways that you and your team can give back in a way that's fun, fulfilling, and sincere. Here are just a few ideas. Brainstorm others with your team.
  o Collect toys to bring to kids in the hospital.
  o Visit a nursing home.
  o Mentor a child.
  o Adopt a school in your neighborhood.
  o Donate clothing.
  o Sponsor a food drive for a local food bank.

[49:1] Fredrickson, Barbara (2008). *Positivity: Groundbreaking Research Reveals How to Embrace the Hidden Strength of Positive Emotions, Overcome Negativity, and Thrive.* Crown Archetype.

[49:2] Achor, Shawn (2010). *The Happiness Advantage: The Seven Principles of Positive Psychology That Fuel Success and Performance at Work.* Crown Business.
[49:3] *The Social Capital Community Benchmark Survey.* Retrieved from: https://www.hks.harvard.edu/saguaro/communitysurvey/
[49:4] Kralik, John (2010). *365 Thank Yous: The Year a Simple Act of Daily Gratitude Changed my Life.* Hyperion.

## ADDITIONAL RESOURCES

*Brain Rules: 12 Principles for Surviving and Thriving at Work, Home, and School,* by John Medina.

*Lesson 50*

● ● ● ●

## THIS IS YOUR LIFE. LIVE IT.

*We shall not cease from exploration*
*And the end of all our exploring*
*Will be to arrive where we started*
*And know the place for the first time.*

*– T.S. ELIOT*

Well, here we are at Lesson 50. We've covered a lot of ground together, yet this is just the beginning. There are more lessons to be learned and lived. I'm hoping that you've had the opportunity to read all 50 Lessons, and begin to apply them to your practice and your life. But if you haven't, not to worry. Focus on what resonates with you. And most importantly – I cannot stress this enough – live the lessons. By that, I mean take action. Do something. Remember Lesson 2. Understand the difference between knowing and doing. Start doing. Talking about what you want to do, and thinking about what you want to do, and writing plans about what you want to do, isn't enough. Those things will not create the life you want to live. To create the life you want – something has got to get done, and someone has got to do it. You. Here's to the journey!

Need some inspiration to get you moving? Here's a collection of quotes from the lessons.

*The future depends on what we do in the present.*

*— Gandhi*

*The goal is not to speculate about what might happen, but to imagine what you can make happen.*

*— Gary Hamel*

*Being busy does not always mean real work. The object of all work is production or accomplishment and to either of these ends there must be forethought, system, planning, intelligence, and honest purpose, as well as perspiration. Seeming to do is not doing.*

*— Thomas A. Edison*

*It's not enough to be busy. So are the ants. The question is: What are we busy about?*

*— Henry David Thoreau*

*Insanity is doing the same thing, over and over again, and expecting different results.*

*— Albert Einstein*

*We are what we repeatedly do. Excellence, then, is not an act but a habit.*

*— Aristotle*

*That's been one of my mantras — focus and simplicity. Simple can be harder than complex: You have to work hard to get your thinking clean to make it simple. But it's worth it in the end because once you get there, you can move mountains.*

— STEVE JOBS

*To be prepared is half the victory.*

— MIGUEL DE CERVANTES

*Things which matter most must never be at the mercy of things which matter least.*

— GOETHE

*Every passing minute is another chance to turn it all around.*

— CAMERON CROWE

*Sleep, riches, and health, to be truly enjoyed, must be interrupted.*

— JEAN PAUL RICHTER

*People who enjoy meetings should not be in charge of anything.*

— THOMAS SOWELL

*Most people haven't realized how out of control their head is when they get 300 e-mails a day.*

— DAVID ALLEN

*Time = Life. Therefore, waste your time and waste your life, or master your time and master your life.*

— *ALAN LAKEIN*

*Simplicity boils down to two steps: Identify the essential. Eliminate the rest.*

— *LEO BABAUTA*

*Why have great talent if you're not going to use it?*

— *DIANE THOMPSON*

*There was nothing like a Saturday — unless it was the Saturday leading up to the last week of school and into summer vacation. That of course was all the Saturdays of your life rolled into one big shiny ball.*

— *NORA ROBERTS*

*Take a rest; a field that has rested gives a bountiful crop.*

— *OVID*

*The purest treasure mortal times can afford is a spotless reputation.*

— *WILLIAM SHAKESPEARE*

*Marketing takes a day to learn. Unfortunately, it takes a lifetime to master.*

— *PHILIP KOTLER*

*A brand is a person's gut feeling about a
product, service or company.*

*— MARTY NEUMEIER*

*Motivation is what gets you started.
Habit is what keeps you going.*

*— JIM ROHN*

*There are no magic wands, no hidden tricks and no secret
handshakes that can bring you immediate success, but with
time, energy and determination, you can get there.*

*— DARREN ROWSE*

*Planning is bringing the future into the present
so you can do something about it now.*

*— ALAN LAKEIN*

*Treasure your relationships, not your possessions.*

*— ANTHONY J. D'ANGELO*

*The greatest compliment that was ever paid
me was when one asked me what I thought,
and attended to my answer.*

*— HENRY DAVID THOREAU*

*People don't buy what you do, they buy why you do it.*

*— SIMON SINEK*

*Money without meaning is not enough compensation.*

*— RODD WAGNER*

*The deepest principle in human nature
is the craving to be appreciated.*

*— WILLIAM JAMES*

*Positivity doesn't just change the contents of your
mind, trading bad thoughts for good ones; it also
changes the scope or boundaries of your mind. It
widens the span of possibilities that you see.*

*— BARBARA FREDRICKSON*

*I believe in intuitions and inspirations...I sometimes
feel that I am right. I do not know that I am.*

*— ALBERT EINSTEIN*

*The best way to predict the future is to invent it.*

*— ALAN KAY*

You can do this. Get started. Your life is waiting for you.

Made in the USA
Lexington, KY
17 May 2017